DEMONIC MNEMONICS

800 Spelling Tricks
for 800 Tricky Words

Murray Suid

Fearon Teacher Aids
Torrance, California
A Division of Frank Schaffer Publications, Inc.

This book is for Ron Harris.

Illustrator: Jim M'Guinness

ISBN-0-8224-6464-0
Library of Congress Catalog Card Number: 80-82982
Printed in the United States of America.

Introduction

The Problem

English spelling is weird (or is it *wierd?*). For almost every rule-abiding word—*mat, cat, sat*—there's a demon whose spelling makes little or no sense.

Some demons have silent letters: si**g**n, **h**erb, **k**nee. Others seem to be missing letters: *welcome* (instead of *wellcome*).

There are demon pairs—words that sound alike but have different spellings—*pain* and *pane*, *Mary* and *marry*. Other pairs are pronounced differently but spelled confusingly alike—*dessert* and *desert*, *hoped* and *hopped*.

What about suffix pairs like **-ance** and **-ence**? They mean the same thing. They're pronounced alike. But there's no rule to tell which suffix to use with a particular word. The same is true for **-able** and **-ible**.

The Solution

Conventional wisdom recommends drilling such demons into submission. Unfortunately, most people can list dozens of words they've studied and looked up again and again, yet they're still not sure of the correct spelling.

A more powerful way to defeat a demon word is to confront it with a *mnemonic* (nĭ–'mahn–ick) device. A mnemonic is a memory trick. It works by creating an association or link between the demon word and an easy-to-spell word or phrase. You may know some mnemonics already. A few are classics:

The school princi**pal** is your **pal**. The princi**ple** that serves as a guideline is a ru**le**.

A station**a**ry, unmoving object st**a**nds still. The station**e**ry that you write letters on is pap**er**.

Mnemonics are sometimes silly, farfetched, or downright outrageous. So much the better, as long as they do their job—to help you master words that are equally outrageous and irrational in the ways they are spelled.

This Book

Demonic Mnemonics offers memory tricks for more than 800 of the most commonly misspelled words. Entries were chosen from a dozen lists of demon words and also from the suggestions of teachers, writers, and editors.

Each entry has three parts. The first part is the *definition*. Knowing what the word means is especially important when dealing with homonyms (*capital* and *capitol*) or other frequently confused pairs (*desert* and *dessert*). Rather than formal, dictionary-type definitions, informal definitions are given so that each word is readily identifiable.

Next comes the *trouble spot*. Boldface type highlights the letter or letters that cause the spelling problem. Awareness of the tricky part of the word strengthens the mnemonic link. When the boldface type alone isn't enough to explain the problem, a parenthetical comment provides clarification.

The third part is the *trick*, the mnemonic device intended to find a permanent niche in your memory, so you'll never misspell that demon again.

Sample Entry

fundamental: basic
    trouble spot: fund**a**mental
    trick: Saying "**amen**" is fund**amen**tal.

In some instances, one of the rules found at the back of this book relates to the tricky spelling of demon words (see pages 115–124). When that is the case, the rule is noted.

Sample Entry

bookkeeper: one who keeps track of business
transactions
trouble spot: boo**kk**eeper
trick: (Compounders, page 117)

Certain mnemonics are immediately memorable. Many mnemonics don't stick quickly, however, and you may have to look up a mnemonic two or three times before you finally get it. But it's worth the effort. Memorizing a mnemonic is almost always easier than trying to memorize a word whose spelling will continue to elude you.

The Eight Basic Links

As you use *Demonic Mnemonics* you will discover that there are eight basic kinds of links.

1. *The built-in-word link.* Many eccentric words contain easy-to-spell clue words. The mnemonic sentence simply links the demon word to its inner clue word.

You h**ear** with your **ear**.
Forty soldiers stormed the **fort**.

2. *The definitional link.* The meaning of a word can sometimes provide the clue to correct spelling. In such cases, the mnemonic takes the form of a definition.

A b**ea**ch is land by the s**ea**.
A b**ee**ch is a tr**ee**.

3. *The analogous pattern link.* This kind of link usually works best to remind you whether a demon is in fact one word or two.

We will go **all together** or **all separately**.

4. *The story sentence link.* This kind of mnemonic tells a story. Some mnemonics combine several recalcitrant words, all irregular in the same way. By turning the words into a story, you

link them together and have an easier time remembering each one.

> **N**either **lei**sured for**ei**gn counterf**ei**ter could s**ei**ze **ei**ther **wei**rd h**ei**ght without forf**ei**ting prot**ei**n.

That's a strange mouthful, but it's far more memorable than a list of **ei** words that are the exception to the "*I* before *E*" rule.

Another kind of story link states the problem itself in a memorable way:

> Use both **i**'s (eyes) in sk**ii**ng.

5. *The acronym link.* A sentence is invented based on each letter of the demon word. Take *arithmetic*:

> **Arithmetic**: **A r**at **i**n **th**e **h**ouse **m**ight **e**at **t**he **i**ce **c**ream.

Strange but true, many people find mastering this 11-word sentence a fun way to remember that arithmetic has an **e** in it—between the **m** and the **t**.

6. *The pronunciation link.* You can learn how to spell some words by inventing memorable ways of pronouncing—or mispronouncing—them:

> Pronounce *Wednesday* "Wed–nes–day."

Naturally, this kind of exaggerated pronunciation should be used only in private. But note that widespread usage will often transform the pronunciation of a word to conform to its spelling. Many people pronounce the **t** in *often*, and *Webster's New Collegiate Dictionary* now gives that pronunciation legitimate standing.

7. *The etymological link.* This kind of link uses one form of a word to clarify the spelling of another. For example, because it is silent, the **c** in *muscle* sometimes is forgotten, so a helpful mnemonic links *muscle* to the word *muscular* in which the **c** is pronounced.

> If you have **musc**les, you're **musc**ular.

8. *The descriptive link.* This kind of mnemonic simply describes the problem in a succinct, memorable way.

> There's no **x** in **ecstasy**.

Warning!

Demonic Mnemonics is not meant to be read from cover to cover. If spelling drill tests your patience, trying to drill 800 mnemonics into your head will test your sanity—doubly so because many of the mnemonics don't make any conventional sense. The sense they do make is speller's sense.

For best results treat each mnemonic as strong medicine of the last resort. Use mnemonics only with those words that have resisted more conventional attack—careful reading, application of the rules (see pages 115–124), and mild drill.

Inventing Your Own Mnemonics

There are two reasons why you might wish to create your own memory tricks. First, a mnemonic found in this book may simply not work for you. Mnemonics, after all, are more quirky than scientific.

Second, if you're like most people, you will be stumped by some words that everyone else finds simple. Don't be embarrassed. Just invent your own personal demon-slayer. (The author did just that when, after ten years, he still couldn't remember if his mother-in-law spelled her name *Jenny* or *Jennie*. Finally, he linked the woman's maiden name—**Fine**—to her first name—*Jenn***ie**.)

Creating mnemonics takes a bit of brain work, but it's fun. Even intermediate-level children can play the game once they're shown how. (At the dinner table a fifth-grader came up with this mnemonic for remembering where all the l's go in *parallel*: First a pair of l's, then one l.) Mnemonic-making is a good exercise for creative thinking.

The secret to creating mnemonics is being familiar with the eight basic linking patterns. In the beginning, keep them handy, as you would a recipe. If you can't forge one kind of association, try another. Go right down the list until something clicks for you.

You'll also want a good dictionary close by. The etymology and definitions found in an entry often provide the basic material for a mnemonic.

Two working assumptions may prove useful as well.

1. *Anything goes.* Don't shy away from silly or sensational associations. You may even disagree with what your trick sentence says. Suppose you write, "Bu**si**ness is a **sin**." Perhaps you like business. Possibly you own 10,000 shares of IBM. Yet, if "Bu**si**ness is a **sin**" works for you, don't reject it.

2. *More than anything goes.* There can be—and there usually are—many spelling tricks for taming a single demon. Even if at first you succeed, you might want to keep trying. You may come up with another trick that works even better.

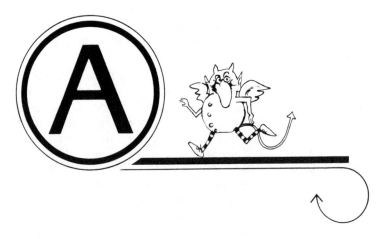

absence: being away
>   trouble spot: abse**n**ce
>   trick: When you **cut** a **c**lass, that's an abse**n**ce.

absolutely: completely
>   trouble spot: abso**lut**ely
>   trick: I abso**lut**ely love **lut**e music.

absorption: soaking up
>   trouble spot: abs**o**r**p**tion
>   trick: When you s**op** something **up**, that's abs**o**r**p**tion.

abundance: great supply
 trouble spot: abun**d**ance
 trick: Food was in abun**dance** at the **dance**.

accelerate: increase speed
 trouble spot: a**cc**elerate
 trick: To a**cc**elerate the **c**able **c**ar, pull this lever.

accident: unexpected happening
 trouble spot: a**cc**ident
 trick: The **c**able **c**ar a**cc**i**dent** made a **dent**.

accidentally: happening by chance
 trouble spot: a**cc**ident**ally**
 trick: The **c**able **c**ar a**cc**ident**ally** ran over **Sally**.

accommodations: lodgings
 trouble spot: a**cc**o**mm**odations
 trick: The a**cc**o**mm**odations were so small that you could measure them in **cc**'s (cubic centimeters) or **mm**'s (millimeters).

account: calculation
 trouble spot: a**cc**ount
 trick: An a**cc**ount is a **c**al**c**ulation.

accumulate: collect
 trouble spot: a**cc**u**m**ulate (one **m**)
 trick: A**cc**u**m**ulate **c**hocolate **c**hips, not **m**oney.

accurate: exact
 trouble spot: a**cc**urate
 trick: Are **c**u**c**koo **c**lo**c**ks a**cc**urate?

accuse: find at fault
 trouble spot: a**cc**use
 trick: I a**cc**use you of eating my **c**hocolate **c**hips.

accustomed: in the habit of
 trouble spot: a**cc**ustomed
 trick: **Tom** is a**cc**us**tom**ed to cable cars.

ache: dull pain
>   trouble spot: a**che**
>   trick: I have **a che**st **ache**.

achievement: accomplishment
>   trouble spot: ach**ieve**ment
>   trick: I was so shy that saying **"Hi Eve"** was a big ach**ieve**ment.

acknowledgment: recognition
>   trouble spot: acknowle**dgm**ent (also *acknowledgement*)
>   trick: The dictionary makes this acknowle**dgm**ent: an **e** or not.

acquaintance: someone known, not a friend
>   trouble spot: a**cqu**aintance
>   trick: Did you **c** (see) the **qu**een's a**cqu**aint**ance** at the **dance**?

acquitted: found innocent
>   trouble spot: a**c**qui**tt**ed
>   trick: I **c** (see) you were a**c**qui**tt**ed of stealing the ki**tt**y.

Did you see the queen's acquaintance at the dance?

acre: measure of land
    trouble spot: ac**re**
    trick: This **acre** is s**acre**d.

across: from one side to the other
    trouble spot: a**cross**
    trick: We took **a cross across** the street.

ad: advertisement
    trouble spot: ad (one **d**; not *add*)
    trick: This **ad** makes me m**ad**.

additional: extra
    trouble spot: a**dd**itional
    trick: I need an **add**itional **D**a**dd**y.

address: place where one lives or gets mail
    trouble spot: a**dd**ress
    trick: **Add** my name to your **add**ress book.

adhesive: sticky substance
    trouble spot: adhesive
    trick: An adhesive is sticky.

adjust: adapt
    trouble spot: a**dj**ust
    trick: When you **adj**ust, you **ad**apt.

advantageous: favorable
    trouble spot: advantag**e**ous
    trick: **Age** is advant**age**ous.

advertise: make known
    trouble spot: advert**ise**
    trick: It's **wise** to advert**ise**.

advice: counsel
    trouble spot: adv**ice** (not *advise*)
    trick: I need adv**ice** about driving on **ice**.

advisable: wise
    trouble spot: advi**sa**ble (no **e** between **s** and **a**)
    trick: Wearing **sable** is advi**sable** in winter.

advise: give advice
>trouble spot: Advise (not *advice*)
>trick: Be **wise** when you ad**vise**.

affect: influence
>trouble spot: **affect** (not *effect*)
>trick: **A**nimals can **a**ffect me.

against: opposed to
>trouble spot: ag**ain**st
>trick: It's hard to **gain** ag**ain**st the wind.

aggravate: make worse or annoy
>trouble spot: a**ggrava**te
>trick: **G**ood grief! **Ava** a**ggrava**tes me.

aide: assistant
>trouble spot: ai**de** (silent **e**; not *aid*)
>trick: An a**ide** is on your **side**.

aisle: passageway
>trouble spot: **ais**le (not *isle*)
>trick: **R**aise the **ais**le.

alcohol: intoxicating liquid
>trouble spot: al**coho**l
>trick: My **coho**rt drinks al**coho**l.

allegiance: loyalty
>trouble spot: a**llegia**nce
>trick: **All** pledge a**llegia**nce to the **giant**.

alley: narrow street
>trouble spot: all**ey**
>trick: Keep your **ey**es on the all**ey**.

allotted: granted
>trouble spot: a**llott**ed
>trick: **All** the b**ott**led water was a**llott**ed.

allowance: money given regularly
>trouble spot: a**llow**ance
>trick: I need **all** my a**llow**ance for the d**ance**.

All pledge allegiance to the giant.

all ready: completely prepared
>trouble spot: **all ready** (two words; not *already*)
>trick: If you're **all ready**, you can **all read**.

all together: as a single group
>trouble spot: **all together** (two words; not *altogether*)
>trick: We will go **all together** or **all separately**.

almost: nearly
>trouble spot: almost (one l)
>trick: I **alm**ost gave **Al** some **alm**s.

a lot: a great deal
>trouble spot: **a lot** (two words; not *alot*)
>trick: You can spend **a little** or **a lot**.

already: earlier
>trouble spot: already (one word; not *all ready*)
>trick: Did **Al al**ready leave?

altar: table for sacred purposes
>trouble spot: alt**ar** (not *alter*)
>trick: An al**tar** is a kind of **ta**ble.

alter: change
    trouble spot: al**ter** (not *altar*)
    trick: Al**ter** the **ter**ms of the contract.

altogether: completely
    trouble spot: a**l**together (one **l**; not *all together*)
    trick: The **alto** sings **alto**gether flat.

always: at all times
    trouble spot: a**l**ways (one **l**)
    trick: **Al** **al**ways wins.

amateur: nonprofessional
    trouble spot: amat**eur**
    trick: Oh, what **a mate u** (you) **r** (are), you **amateur**.

ambitious: eager
    trouble spot: am**bit**ious
    trick: I'm not a **bit** am**bit**ious.

amendment: addition
    trouble spot: a**m**endment (one **m**)
    trick: An a**mend**ment **mend**s the law.

amiable: friendly
    trouble spot: am**i**able
    trick: **Am I able** to be **amiable**?

amount: quantity
    trouble spot: a**m**ount (one **m**)
    trick: The **amount** was less than **a mount**ain.

analyze: separate into parts
    trouble spot: anal**yze**
    trick: **Y** (why) anal**yze** **ze**bras?

angel: supernatural being
    trouble spot: an**gel** (not *angle*)
    trick: **Angel**s are **angel**ic.

angle: shape made when two straight lines meet
    trouble spot: an**gle** (not *angel*)
    trick: The **gl**ider came in at a sharp an**gle**.

annihilate: destroy completely
    trouble spot: an**ni**hilate (one **l**)
    trick: If you say "**Hi**" **late** to **Ann** she will **annihilate** you.

announcement: notice
    trouble spot: an**noun**cement
    trick: **Ann** wrote the **announcement** in **cement**.

annual: yearly
    trouble spot: an**nu**al
    trick: Invite **Ann** to our **ann**ual picnic.

answer: reply
    trouble spot: ans**w**er
    trick: Pronounce *answer* "ans–wer."

antidote: remedy
    trouble spot: ant**id**ote
    trick: I h**id** the ant**id**ote.

'e'y: worry
    ouble spot: an**x**iety
    r' k: **X** out anxiety.

Ann wrote the announcement in cement.

apologize: express regret
    trouble spot: apologize (one **l**)
    trick: A **polo** player shouldn't a**polog**ize for lack of **size**.

apparatus: instruments or equipment
    trouble spot: a**pp**arat**us**
    trick: Does this **app**arat**us** make **us** ha**pp**y?

apparently: evidently
    trouble spot: a**pp**a**rent**ly
    trick: You're **app**a**rent**ly ha**pp**y about the low **rent**.

appearance: act of appearing; how a person or thing seems
    trouble spot: a**pp**ea**rance**
    trick: The band was ha**pp**y to make an **app**ea**rance** at
    the **dance**.

appointment: engagement
    trouble spot: a**pp**ointment
    trick: This is a ha**pp**y a**pp**ointment.

appreciate: think well of
    trouble spot: a**pp**reciate
    trick: I **app**reciate being ha**pp**y.

appropriate: fitting
    trouble spot: a**pp**ropri**ate**
    trick: The **apple** I **ate** was **appropri**ate.

approval: favorable opinion
    trouble spot: a**pp**roval
    trick: Your **app**roval makes me ha**pp**y.

apricot: kind of fruit
    trouble spot: apricot (one **p**)
    trick: Are **apri**cots ripe in **April**?

architect: designer of buildings
    trouble spot: ar**ch**itect
    trick: The **arch**itect designed the **arch**.

arctic: near the North Pole
> trouble spot: arctic
> trick: The arctic is cold.

argument: disagreement
> trouble spot: argument (no **e** between **u** and **m**)
> trick: An ar**gum**ent **gum**s up the works.

arithmetic: science of computing real numbers
> trouble spot: arithmetic
> trick: **Arithmetic: A r**at **i**n **t**he **h**ouse **m**ight **e**at **t**he **i**ce **c**ream.

ascend: go up
> trouble spot: ascend
> trick: As**c**end this **sc**ary hill.

ascertain: make sure
> trouble spot: ascertain
> trick: When you **ascertain** a fact, be **as certain** as you possibly can.

asinine: silly
> trouble spot: asinine (one **s**)
> trick: Is it **a sin** to be **asin**ine?

assassin: killer of an important person
> trouble spot: assassin
> trick: An **assass**in is a double **ass**.

assistant: helper
> trouble spot: assistant
> trick: An **ass** and an **ant** are my **ass**ist**ant**s.

asterisk: starlike mark (*)
> trouble spot: asterisk
> trick: Is there a **risk** in using an aste**risk**?

athlete: person active in a sport
> trouble spot: athlete (no **e** between **h** and **l**)
> trick: After her b**ath let** the **athlet**e rest.

An ass and an ant are my assistants.

attacked: assaulted
>trouble spot: atta**ck**ed (no **t**)
>trick: When they att**acked**, we b**acked** away.

attendance: presence
>trouble spot: at**ten**d**ance**
>trick: **At ten** we'll take at**ten**d**ance** for the **dance**.

attention: notice
>trouble spot: at**ten**tion
>trick: Pay at**ten**tion **at ten**.

attitude: state of mind
>trouble spot: at**ti**tude
>trick: **Batt**le your bad at**ti**tude.

attorney: lawyer
>trouble spot: attorn**eys**
>trick: The attorn**eys** have lost their k**eys**.

Australia: continent in the South Pacific
>trouble spot: Austra**l**ia (no **i** between **a** and **l**)
>trick: **Al** is from cent**ral** Austra**l**ia.

autumn: fall
>trouble spot: autum**n** (silent **n**)
>trick: **N**ovember is the end of autum**n**.

auxiliary: assisting
>trouble spot: auxi**li**ary
>trick: There's a **liar** in the auxi**liar**y group.

awful: terrible
>trouble spot: awful (one **l**)
>trick: **Ul**cers are aw**ful**.

axle: shaft on which a wheel turns
>trouble spot: ax**le**
>trick: They're having an ax**le** sa**le**.

baboon: monkey
>trouble spot: ba**b**oon (one **b**)
>trick: A **bab**oon is like a **bab**y.

bachelor: unmarried man
>trouble spot: b**ach**elor (no **t** between **a** and **c**)
>trick: **Bach** was not a **bach**elor.

baggage: luggage
   trouble spot: ba**gg**age
   trick: **G**et a **g**ood **g**rip on your ba**gg**age.

balance: bring to equilibrium
   trouble spot: balance (one **l**)
   trick: It's hard to b**alance a lance**.

balloon: inflatable rubber bag
   trouble spot: ba**ll**oon
   trick: A **ball**oon is a **ball**.

ballots: papers that register votes
   trouble spot: ba**ll**ots
   trick: **Ball**ots will be counted at the **ball**.

banana: kind of fruit
   trouble spot: ba**na**na
   trick: It's a **no-no** to **ban a na**ked **banana**.

barbecue: party where food is cooked over an open fire
   trouble spot: barbe**cue**
   trick: Summer's our **cue** to hold a barbe**cue**.

bare: without covering
   trouble spot: b**are** (not *bear*)
   trick: Do you **care** if I'm b**are**?

bargain: good buy, agreement
   trouble spot: bar**gain**
   trick: What did you **gain** in that bar**gain**?

basically: fundamentally
   trouble spot: basic**all**y
   trick: Basic**ally**, I trust our **ally**.

basis: foundation
   trouble spot: basis (one **s**)
   trick: **Sis** learned the ba**sis** of mathematics.

bazaar: market
   trouble spot: b**azaa**r (not *bizarre*)
   trick: Our market is called the Triple A **(aaa)** Bazaar.

Our neighbor's eight beige reindeer weighed
too much to send by freight.

bear: large mammal
> trouble spot: b**ear** (not *bare*)
> trick: Did you ever **eat** b**ear** m**eat**?

beautiful: very pretty
> trouble spot: b**eautiful**
> trick: **Beautiful**: **B**oys **e**at **a**pples **u**nder **t**rees **i**n **f**all
> **u**nder **l**eaves.

beggar: person who asks for charity
> trouble spot: begg**ar**
> trick: The begg**ar** came from **far** away.

beginning: start
> trouble spot: begi**nn**ing
> trick: At the begi**nn**ing we stayed at the **inn**.

behavior: actions
> trouble spot: beha**vior**
> trick: Watch out for **vio**lent beha**vior**.

beige: grayish tan
> trouble spot: b**ei**ge
> trick: Our n**ei**ghbor's **ei**ght b**ei**ge r**ei**ndeer w**ei**ghed too
> much to send by fr**ei**ght.

believable: credible
    trouble spot: belie**va**ble (no **e** between **v** and **a**)
    trick: **Eva** is not belie**va**ble.

believe: accept as true
    trouble spot: bel**ie**ve
    trick: Never bel**ie**ve a **lie**.

benefited: got an advantage
    trouble spot: benefited (one **t**)
    trick: My **bite** benefi**te**d from braces.

berserk: state of violent rage
    trouble spot: be**r**serk
    trick: I went **ber**serk in **Ber**lin.

bicycle: two-wheeled vehicle
    trouble spot: bi**c**y**c**le
    trick: Don't ride your bi**cy**cle in **icy** weather.

binoculars: optical device
    trouble spot: bi**n**oculars (one **n**)
    trick: The **bin**oculars are in the **bin**.

bizarre: odd
    trouble spot: b**izarre** (not *bazaar*)
    trick: It was another **bizarre** show **biz arre**st.

blizzard: violent storm
    trouble spot: bli**zz**ard
    trick: You won't find a buzzard buzzing in a blizzard.

bookkeeper: one who keeps track of business transactions
    trouble spot: boo**kk**eeper
    trick: (Compounders, page 117)

bought: purchased
    trouble spot: b**ough**t
    trick: I th**ough**t I'd b**ough**t en**ough cough** syrup to make it thr**ough** this **rough**, **tough** winter.

boulevard: wide street
    trouble spot: b**ou**levard
    trick: This **bou**levard is **out** of **bou**nds.

boundary: edge
    trouble spot: bound**a**ry
    trick: M**a**ry's lamb crossed the bound**a**ry of the school g**a**rden.

brake: device for slowing or stopping a vehicle
    trouble spot: br**ake** (not *break*)
    trick: For heaven's s**ake**, use the br**ake**!

breadth: width
    trouble spot: brea**d**th (not *breath*)
    trick: The **bread** has **bread**th.

break: cause to come apart
    trouble spot: br**eak** (not *brake*)
    trick: **Break bread** with me.

breathe: take air into the lungs and then let it out
    trouble spot: breath**e** (not *breath*)
    trick: Breath**e** with **e**ase.

brilliant: outstanding
    trouble spot: bri**lli**ant
    trick: The Three Stooges were bri**lli**ant with si**lli**ness.

bruise: injure
    trouble spot: br**ui**se
    trick: A br**ui**se can r**ui**n fr**ui**t.

budget: plan for matching income to outgo
    trouble spot: bu**dg**et
    trick: **Bud**, don't **budg**e from your **budg**et.

built: constructed
    trouble spot: b**ui**lt
    trick: Have you any g**ui**lt about what **u** (you) and **I** b**ui**lt?

buoy: floating object
    trouble spot: b**uo**y (not *boy*)
    trick: A b**uo**y warns of **u**nderwater **o**bjects.

burglar: thief
>   trouble spot: bur**gl**ar
>   trick: A bur**glar** commits **lar**ceny.

business: a company
>   trouble spot: bu**si**ness
>   trick: Bu**si**ness is a **sin**.

buzzard: kind of bird
>   trouble spot: bu**zz**ard
>   trick: You won't find a buzzard buzzing in a blizzard.

cafeteria: self-service restaurant
>   trouble spot: ca**fe**teria
>   trick: Is it s**afe** to eat in the c**afe**teria?

calendar: chart of the days of the year
>   trouble spot: calen**dar**
>   trick: The calen**dar** is a list of **da**tes.

callous: lacking pity
>   trouble spot: ca**llou**s (not *callus*)
>   trick: Don't **call out** to a **callou**s person for help.

callus: hardened patch of skin
    trouble spot: ca**llu**s (not *callous*)
    trick: **Call us** if you have a **callus**.

campaign: series of planned actions
    trouble spot: campai**g**n (silent **g**)
    trick: Campai**g**n for clean **g**overnment.

cancel: do away with
    trouble spot: canc**el**
    trick: Can**cel** the **cel**ebration.

candidate: person running for an elective office
    trouble spot: can**di**date
    trick: Was the **candid**ate **candid**?

cannon: large, mounted piece of artillery
    trouble spot: ca**nn**on (not *canon*)
    trick: **Ann canno**t fire the **canno**n.

canoe: narrow, light boat
    trouble spot: can**oe**
    trick: This can**oe** leaks like a sh**oe**.

canvas: closely woven, coarse cloth
    trouble spot: canva**s** (one **s**; not *canvass*)
    trick: The circus was in a **vas**t can**vas** tent.

canvass: survey
    trouble spot: canva**ss** (not *canvas*)
    trick: Let's canv**ass** the m**ass** of people.

capacity: amount of room or space inside
    trouble spot: capa**ci**ty
    trick: What is the capa**city** of this **city** for tourists?

capital: uppercase letter
    trouble spot: capit**al** (not *capitol*)
    trick: **A** is the first capit**al** letter.

capital: government city
    trouble spot: capit**al** (not *capitol*)
    trick: There's a lot of **tal**k in the capi**tal** city.

This canoe leaks like a shoe.

capital: money used to run a business
    trouble spot: capit**al** (not *capitol*)
    trick: **C**ash is a form of capit**al**.

capitol: building where a legislature meets
    trouble spot: capit**ol** (not *capital*)
    trick: The capit**ol** building has a d**o**me.

captain: commanding officer
    trouble spot: capt**ain**
    trick: The capt**ain** is the m**ain** officer.

career: life work
    trouble spot: car**eer**
    trick: She made a car**eer** selling b**eer**.

carrying: taking from one place to another
    trouble spot: carr**y**ing
    trick: (Y-Enders, page 123)

cavalry: troops on horses
    trouble spot: ca**val**ry
    trick: The ca**val**ry soldiers were **val**iant.

cemetery: burial place
    trouble spot: c**e**m**e**t**e**ry
    trick: Life in a c**e**m**e**t**e**ry is all **e**'s (ease).

cereal: breakfast food
> trouble spot: **c**ereal (not *serial*)
> trick: **C**ornflakes **cereal** is **real** good.

certain: sure
> trouble spot: cert**ain**
> trick: Is the capt**ain** cert**ain** it will **rain**?

changeable: not staying the same
> trouble spot: chang**e**able
> trick: You should always be **able** to keep the **change** in **changeable**.

changing: becoming something else
> trouble spot: chan**gi**ng (no **e** between **g** and **i**)
> trick: When something is **hanging** it can't be **changing**.

chaperon: person who supervises another person or persons
> trouble spot: **ch**aperon (also spelled *chaperone*)
> trick: My **chap**eron is a good **chap**.

chateau: large country house
> trouble spot: chat**eau**
> trick: After **tea u** (you) can visit my chat**eau**.

chauffeur: driver of an automobile
> trouble spot: chau**ffeur**
> trick: Our chau**ffeur** hates the traffic in **Eur**ope.

chief: leader
> trouble spot: ch**ie**f
> trick: **Hi, chief.**

chocolate: food made from cocoa beans
> trouble spot: cho**col**ate
> trick: I like **cola** better than cho**cola**te.

choose: select
> trouble spot: cho**o**se (not *chose*)
> trick: What would a **loose goose** ch**oo**se?

chose: past tense of *choose*
 trouble spot: ch**o**se (not *choose*)
 trick: My n**ose** ch**ose** this r**ose**.

Cincinnati: city in Ohio
 trouble spot: Ci**nci**n**n**ati
 trick: We stayed **in** the **inn** at **C**incinnati.

clientele: customers
 trouble spot: clien**tele**
 trick: Our clien**tele** reach us by **tele**phone.

clothes: wearing apparel
 trouble spot: cl**o**th**es** (not *cloths*)
 trick: Wear your **other** cl**othe**s.

college: school of higher learning
 trouble spot: col**l**ege
 trick: If you want to go to co**llege**, eat **all** your v**ege**tables.

colonel: chief officer of a regiment
 trouble spot: co**lone**l (pronounced *kernel*)
 trick: Are you the **lone** co**lone**l?

Are you the lone colonel?

colossal: huge
    trouble spot: colossal (one **l**)
    trick: This was a colossal **loss**.

coma: unconsciousness
    trouble spot: coma (one **m**; not *comma*)
    trick: Will the patient **come** out of the **coma**?

comfortable: providing ease
    trouble spot: comfortable
    trick: The **fort** has a comfortable **table**.

coming: approaching
    trouble spot: coming (no **e** between **m** and **i**)
    trick: They're coming home in a **minute**.

comma: punctuation mark (,)
    trouble spot: comma (not *coma*)
    trick: **Comma** errors are **common**.

commercial: advertisement
    trouble spot: commercial
    trick: Here's a commercial for **m&m's**®

commission: group of people doing work for the government
    trouble spot: commission
    trick: A commission doubles the work—and the letters **mm** and **ss**.

committee: group of people working together
    trouble spot: committee
    trick: A committee doubles the work—and the letters **mm**, **tt**, and **ee**.

communication: means of sending information
    trouble spot: communication
    trick: **Mass media** are used in communication.

community: people living as a group
    trouble spot: community
    trick: We're a summer community.

comparatively: relatively
>   trouble spot: comparatively
>   trick: The **rat** is comparatively bright.

comparison: estimation of similarities and differences
>   trouble spot: comparison
>   trick: **Paris** is beyond com**paris**on.

compatible: going together
>   trouble spot: compatible
>   trick: Is science compat**ible** with the **Bible**?

compelled: forced
>   trouble spot: compelled
>   trick: I was com**pell**ed to s**pell** the word correctly.

competent: capable
>   trouble spot: competent
>   trick: **Compete**nt people **compete**.

competition: contest
>   trouble spot: competition
>   trick: I'm entering my **pet** in the com**pet**ition.

complacent: smug
>   trouble spot: complacent
>   trick: I'm com**place**nt about my **place** in life.

complement: something that completes
>   trouble spot: complement (not *compliment*)
>   trick: A **comple**ment **comple**tes.

completely: totally
>   trouble spot: completely
>   trick: **Pete** comp**lete**ly did it.

complexion: appearance
>   trouble spot: complexion
>   trick: I have a **complex complex**ion.

compliment: expression of approval
>   trouble spot: compliment (not *complement*)
>   trick: I **like** compl**i**ments.

compromise: give up something in order to agree
    trouble spot: compromise
    trick: Be **wise**, compromise.

conceive: imagine
    trouble spot: conceive
    trick: **Once I've** done something, I can **conceive** of it.

condemn: pass an adverse judgment
    trouble spot: condemn (silent **n**)
    trick: When you condemn, you express condemnation.

confidence: trust
    trouble spot: confidence
    trick: I have confidence in the **fence**.

Connecticut: U.S. state
    trouble spot: Connecticut
    trick: **Connect** with **Connect**icut.

conscience: sense of right and wrong
    trouble spot: conscience
    trick: Does **science** have a con**science**?

consensus: agreement
    trouble spot: consensus
    trick: **Send us** the consensus you have reached.

nsistent: always the same
    trouble spot: consistent
    trick: This **tent** gives us consis**tent** protection.

consul: government official
    trouble spot: consul (not *council* or *counsel*)
    trick: **Consul**t with the **consul**.

contemptible: deserving scorn
    trouble spot: contemptible
    trick: The **Bible** says sin is contempti**ble**

continually: going on without interruption
    trouble spot: continually
    trick: **Sally** is continu**ally** helping me.

The troll controlled the bridge.

control: restraint
    trouble spot: contro**l** (one **l**)
    trick: Practice self-contro**l**.

controlled: directed
    trouble spot: contro**ll**ed
    trick: The **troll** con**troll**ed the bridge.

convenience: anything that makes things easy
    trouble spot: conven**ience**
    trick: Sc**ience** is a conven**ience**.

cooperate: work in harmony
    trouble spot: c**oo**perate
    trick: Hens **coop**erate in the **coop**.

cord: thick string or rope
    trouble spot: **cor**d (not *chord*)
    trick: Tie the **cor**k with the **cor**d.

cordial: friendly
    trouble spot: cord**ial**
    trick: After you **dial**, speak in a cor**dial** voice.

corduroy: heavy cotton fabric
trouble spot: cord**u**roy
trick: Cord**ur**oy is **dur**able.

corps: group of workers or soldiers
trouble spot: cor**ps** (silent **p** and **s**; not *corpse*)
trick: The cor**ps** has ca**ps**.

corpse: dead body
trouble spot: corps**e** (not *corps*)
trick: You'll **end** as a corps**e**.

correspondence: communication by letters
trouble spot: co**rr**espond**e**nce
trick: I hu**rr**y my co**rr**espon**den**ce by writing in my **den**.

corroborate: confirm
trouble spot: co**rr**o**b**orate
trick: Don't **worry**, I'll co**rr**oborate your story.

cough: sudden expulsion of air from lungs
trouble spot: c**ough**
trick: I th**ough**t I'd b**ough**t en**ough** c**ough** syrup to make it thr**ough** this r**ough**, t**ough** winter.

council: legislative body
trouble spot: coun**ci**l (not *counsel* or *consul*)
trick: The **ci**ty coun**ci**l is a group of **ci**tizens.

counsel: give advice
trouble spot: coun**sel** (not *council* or *consul*)
trick: Coun**sel sel**dom.

counterfeiter: person who makes phony money
trouble spot: counterf**ei**ter
trick: N**ei**ther l**ei**sured for**ei**gn counterf**ei**ter could s**ei**ze **ei**ther w**ei**rd h**ei**ght without forf**ei**ting prot**ei**n.

courageous: brave
trouble spot: cour**age**ous
trick: In this **age**, being cour**age**ous counts.

course: way
>   trouble spot: co**ur**se (not *coarse*)
>   trick: We've lost **our** co**ur**se.

courteous: polite
>   trouble spot: **cour**teous
>   trick: Be **court**eous in **court**.

criticism: informed judgment
>   trouble spot: criti**ci**sm
>   trick: A **critic** writes **critic**ism.

criticize: analyze the worth of a work
>   trouble spot: criti**ci**ze
>   trick: The **critic** won't **criticize** the prize.

curiosity: interest
>   trouble spot: curio**sity**
>   trick: Curio**sity** doesn't **sit** still.

curriculum: course of studies
>   trouble spot: cu**rr**iculum
>   trick: Don't h**urr**y through the cu**rr**iculum.

customer: patron
>   trouble spot: cust**omer**
>   trick: **H**omer is a good cust**omer**.

cylinder: chamber in an engine
>   trouble spot: cyli**nder**
>   trick: An i**cy cylinder** will h**inder** an engine.

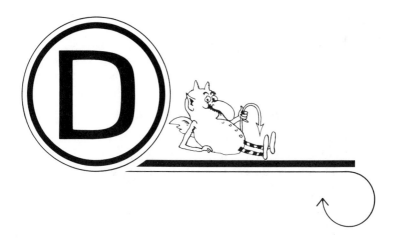

deceive: mislead
    trouble spot: dec**ei**ve
    trick: (*I* before *E*, page 120)

decent: good
    trouble spot: de**c**ent (not *descent*)
    trick: Re**cent**ly you've been **decent**.

defendant: the accused in a legal case
    trouble spot: defend**a**nt
    trick: The defend**ant** was an **ant**.

democracy: a system of government
    trouble spot: democra**c**y
    trick: Democ**racy** is **racy**.

dependent: relying on
    trouble spot: depend**e**nt
    trick: I'm depend**ent** on you for my **rent**.

descent: downward slope
    trouble spot: de**sc**ent (not *decent*)
    trick: Begin the **sc**ary de**sc**ent.

describe: tell or write about
    trouble spot: de**s**cribe
    trick: **De**scribe the **de**sign.

description: picture in words
>   trouble spot: descri**p**tion
>   trick: The **scr**ipt gives a detailed de**scr**iption of the t**rip**

desert: dry region
>   trouble spot: de**s**ert (one **s**; not *dessert*)
>   trick: The desert is filled with **s**and.

desert: reward or punishment
>   trouble spot: de**s**ert (one **s**; not *dessert*)
>   trick: A just **desert** is what you **deser**ve.

desirable: worth wanting
>   trouble spot: desirable (no **e** between **r** and **a**)
>   trick: Are **rab**ies desi**rab**le?

despair: hopelessness
>   trouble spot: de**s**pair
>   trick: I feel **des**pair when I sit at my **des**k.

desperate: hopeless
>   trouble spot: desp**erate**
>   trick: I **rate** you desp**erate**.

despise: hate
>   trouble spot: desp**ise**
>   trick: It's not **wise** to desp**ise**.

dessert: sweet ending of a meal
>   trouble spot: de**ss**ert (not *desert*)
>   trick: Strawberry shortcake is my favorite· dessert.

destroy: ruin
>   trouble spot: d**e**stroy
>   trick: **De**finitely **de**stroy **de**mons.

develop: bring to fruition
>   trouble spot: develo**p** (no **e** at the end)
>   trick: Develo**p** until you sto**p**.

development: outcome of some action
>   trouble spot: develo**pm**ent (no **e** between **p** and **m**)
>   trick: Let's discuss this develo**pm**ent in the **P.M.**

Definitely destroy demons.

dictionary: book of words
>trouble spot: diction**ary**
>trick: **Mary** reads the diction**ary**.

difference: unlikeness or space between persons or things
>trouble spot: di**ff**er**e**nce
>trick: What's the **difference** if we **differ** in the **en**d?

difficult: hard to do or understand
>trouble spot: di**ff**icult
>trick: The two **f**'s are doubly di**ff**icult.

dilemma: predicament
>trouble spot: di**lemm**a (one **l**, two **m**'s)
>trick: **Let**'s help **Emma** with her di**lemma**.

dining: eating
>trouble spot: di**n**ing (one **n**)
>trick: This is **fine dini**ng.

disappear: vanish
>trouble spot: di**s**a**pp**ear
>trick: Th**is app**le di**sapp**ears.

disastrous: calamitous
>trouble spot: disas**tr**ous (no **e** between **t** and **r**)
>trick: The **astro**naut's crash was dis**astro**us.

discipline: branch of learning; rules of behavior
   trouble spot: di**sci**pline
   trick: The di**sci**pline of **sci**ence draws no **line**s.

discuss: talk over
   trouble spot: discu**ss**
   trick: Don't f**uss**; just disc**uss**.

dissatisfied: not pleased
   trouble spot: di**ss**atisfied
   trick: (Nay-Sayers, page 121)

divided: parted
   trouble spot: di**vi**ded
   trick: My **divi**ng **divi**ded the water.

divine: terrific
   trouble spot: di**vi**ne
   trick: **Divi**ng's **divi**ne.

doctor: a physician
   trouble spot: doct**or**
   trick: Follow the doct**or's or**ders.

does: accomplishes
   trouble spot: d**oes**
   trick: D**oes** she put her t**oes** in her sh**oes**?

doesn't: contraction of *does not*
   trouble spot: does**n't**
   trick: (Contract'ns, page 117)

dominant: controlling
   trouble spot: domin**ant**
   trick: The queen **ant** is domin**ant**.

don't: contraction of *do not*
   trouble spot: do**n't**
   trick: (Contract'ns, page 117)

dormitory: rooms for sleeping
   trouble spot: dormitory
   trick: I live in the dor**mit**ory at **MIT**.

drunkenness: state of being drunk
  trouble spot: drunke**nn**ess
  trick: (*Ness*-Enders, page 122)

dyeing: process of coloring with dye
  trouble spot: dy**e**ing (not *dying*)
  trick: When **dyeing**, leave the **dye in**.

dying: process of giving up life
  trouble spot: dying (not *dyeing*)
  trick: When there's d**ying**, there's cr**ying**.

easel: tripod to hold an artist's canvas
  trouble spot: eas**e**l
  trick: This **easel** goes up with **ease**.

ecstasy: great delight
  trouble spot: **ecs**tasy (no **x**)
  trick: There's no **x** in **ecstasy.**

effect: bring about
  trouble spot: **e**ffect (not *affect*)
  trick: It takes **eff**ort to **eff**ect **e**nthusiasm.

Neither leisured foreign counterfeiter could seize either weird height without forfeiting protein.

eighth: the one after *seventh*
   trouble spot: eigh**th**
   trick: **Eight + h = eighth**.

either: one or the other of two
   trouble spot: **ei**ther
   trick: N**ei**ther l**ei**sured for**ei**gn count**er**f**ei**ter could s**ei**ze **ei**ther w**ei**rd h**ei**ght without forf**ei**ting prot**ei**n.

eligible: qualified
   trouble spot: eli**gi**ble
   trick: Though the rules are **rigi**d, you're el**igi**ble.

embarrassing: making self-conscious
   trouble spot: emba**rr**a**ss**ing
   trick: It's doubly emba**rr**a**ss**ing to forget the double **r (rr)** and double **s (ss)** in emba**rr**a**ss**ing.

eminent: famous
   trouble spot: em**in**ent
   trick: **Mine** is the most em**ine**nt family.

emphasize: stress
   trouble spot: empha**size**
   trick: Skyscrapers empha**size size**.

endeavor: task
>   trouble spot: end**eavo**r
>   trick: A h**eavy** end**eavo**r takes eff**or**t.

enemy: foe
>   trouble spot: **ene**my
>   trick: My **ene**my has **ene**rgy.

engineer: train operator
>   trouble spot: engin**ee**r
>   trick: An engin**ee**r must s**ee** and st**eer**.

enormous: huge
>   trouble spot: enorm**ou**s
>   trick: A th**ou**sand p**ou**nds is an enorm**ou**s am**ou**nt.

enough: sufficient
>   trouble spot: en**ough**
>   trick: I th**ough**t I'd b**ough**t en**ough** c**ough** syrup to make it thr**ough** the r**ough**, t**ough** winter.

enterprise: venture
>   trouble spot: enterprise
>   trick: Chart the **rise** of free enterp**rise**.

envelope: container for a letter
>   trouble spot: envelop**e** (not *envelop*)
>   trick: Even a d**ope** can seal an envel**ope**.

environment: surroundings
>   trouble spot: envi**ron**ment
>   trick: **Ron** values his envi**ron**ment.

equipment: tools needed for a job
>   trouble spot: equipment (one **p**)
>   trick: What equi**pment** came with this sh**ipment**?

equipped: supplied
>   trouble spot: equipped
>   trick: This car was fully equi**pped** when sh**ipped**.

essential: necessary
>trouble spot: **ess**ential
>trick: Is this m**ess ess**ential?

evidently: clear, obvious
>trouble spot: eviden**tly** (no **al** between **t** and **l**)
>trick: Eviden**tly** the answer will shor**tly** appear.

exaggerate: magnify beyond the facts
>trouble spot: exa**gg**erate
>trick: **G**ood **g**rief! How you exa**gg**erate!

exceed: go beyond
>trouble spot: ex**cee**d
>trick: There's no ex**cu**se when you **exceed** the safe sp**eed.**

excellent: first class
>trouble spot: ex**c**ellent
>trick: We have an ex**c**ellent ex**cu**se.

except: other than
>trouble spot: ex**c**ept (not *accept*)
>trick: There's no ex**cu**se ex**c**ept illness.

exercise: activity
>trouble spot: ex**er**cise (no **c** between **x** and **e**)
>trick: It's **wise** to **exer**t yourself when you **exercise.**

exhausted: tired out
>trouble spot: ex**h**austed (silent **h**)
>trick: I was so **exha**usted, I **exha**led noisily.

existence: life
>trouble spot: exis**tence**
>trick: It went out of exis**tence ten** years ago.

expense: cost
>trouble spot: ex**pense**
>trick: The **pens** are an extra ex**pens**e.

explanation: reason
>trouble spot: expla**n**ation (contrast with *explain*)
>trick: This **plan** calls for an ex**plan**ation.

extension: going beyond
    trouble spot: exten**s**ion
    trick: Pull the ex**tens**ion cord **tense**.

extraordinary: unusual
    trouble spot: extr**a**ordinary
    trick: Pronounce *extraordinary* "extra–ordinary."

extreme: drastic
    trouble spot: extr**eme**
    trick: We'll have to try an ext**reme reme**dy.

familiar: intimate
    trouble spot: famil**iar**
    trick: A **liar** has to be fami**liar** with the facts.

fascinating: intriguing
    trouble spot: fas**c**inating
    trick: **Sc**ary things can be fas**c**inating.

February: second month of the year
    trouble spot: Feb**r**uary
    trick: **Br**other, it's cold in Feb**r**uary.

fertile: rich in resources
    trouble spot: fert**ile**
    trick: The **Nile** valley is fert**ile**.

fiend: evil person
    trouble spot: f**ie**nd
    trick: **Fie** on you, f**ie**nd.

fiery: hot
    trouble spot: f**ie**ry
    trick: You can d**ie** in a f**ie**ry crash.

finally: at last
    trouble spot: fin**ally**
    trick: S**ally** fin**ally** came home.

flammable: easily set on fire
    trouble spot: fla**mm**able
    trick: Trees are more fla**mm**able in su**mm**er.

flannel: kind of cloth
    trouble spot: fla**nnel**
    trick: Don't wear fla**nnel** in a tu**nnel**.

flies: moves through the air
    trouble spot: fl**ies**
    trick: A **lie** fl**ies**.

forehead: part of the face
    trouble spot: **fore**head
    trick: Your **fore**head goes be**fore**.

foreign: from another country; unusual
    trouble spot: for**ei**gn
    trick: N**ei**ther l**ei**sured for**ei**gn counterf**ei**ter could s**ei**ze **ei**ther w**ei**rd h**ei**ght without forf**ei**ting protein.

forest: tree-covered land
    trouble spot: fo**r**est (one **r**)
    trick: Where is the **rest** of the fo**rest**?

Don't wear flannel in a tunnel.

foreword: preface
> trouble spot: fore**word** (not *forward*)
> trick: **Word**s be**fore** make a **foreword**.

forfeiting: losing
> trouble spot: forf**ei**ting
> trick: N**ei**ther l**ei**sured for**ei**gn counterf**ei**ter could s**ei**ze
> **ei**ther w**ei**rd h**ei**ght without forf**ei**ting prot**ei**n.

forgotten: not remembered
> trouble spot: for**gotten**
> trick: I **got ten** things, but I've for**gotten** what they are.

forth: onward
> trouble spot: for**th** (not *fourth*)
> trick: Go **forth** from the **fort**.

forty: a number
> trouble spot: for**ty**
> trick: **Fort**y soldiers stormed the **fort**.

forward: toward the front
    trouble spot: **forward** (not *foreword*)
    trick: All those **for war**, step **forward**.

fourth: the one after *third*
    trouble spot: **four**th (not *forth*)
    trick: The **four**th number is **four**.

Frances: a girl's name
    trouble spot: Franc**es** (not *Francis*)
    trick: Franc**es** is **her** name; Franc**is** is **his** name.

Francis: a boy's name
    trouble spot: Franc**is** (not *Frances*)
    trick: Franc**is** is **his** name; Franc**es** is **her** name.

freight: material transported
    trouble spot: fr**ei**ght
    trick: Our n**ei**ghbor's **eight** b**ei**ge r**ei**ndeer w**ei**ghed too much to send by fr**ei**ght.

friend: a person one knows well and cares for
    trouble spot: fr**ie**nd
    trick: A fr**ie**nd won't **lie**.

fulfill: carry out
    trouble spot: fulfill (also spelled *fulfil*)
    trick: The **elf will** ful**fill** your wish.

fundamental: basic
    trouble spot: fund**a**mental
    trick: Saying **"amen"** is fund**amen**tal.

furniture: chairs, tables
    trouble spot: furnit**ure**
    trick: It s**ure** is lovely furnit**ure**.

further: beyond, to a greater degree
    trouble spot: fur**ther**
    trick: Don't h**ur**t me any fur**ther**.

gallon: measure equal to four quarts
  trouble spot: ga**ll**on
  trick: **All** we need is a ga**ll**on of gas.

genius: brilliant person
  trouble spot: gen**ius** (no **o** between **i** and **u**)
  trick: **I** before **us** ends every gen**ius**.

gentleman: gracious man
  trouble spot: gent**lem**an
  trick: The gent**lem**an ordered a **lem**on.

genuine: authentic
  trouble spot: genuin**e**
  trick: This **wine** is genu**ine**.

glimpsed: viewed
  trouble spot: glim**ps**ed
  trick: I glim**ps**ed the ecli**ps**e before I colla**ps**ed.

gnarled: knotted
  trouble spot: **gn**arled (silent **g**)
  trick: The **gn**arled **gn**ome **gn**ashed his teeth as he **gn**awed a **gn**at.

The gnarled gnome gnashed his teeth as he gnawed a gnat.

gnashed: ground
> trouble spot: **gn**ashed (silent **g**)
> trick: The **gn**arled **gn**ome **gn**ashed his teeth as he **gn**awed a **gn**at.

gnat: tiny two-winged insect
> trouble spot: **gn**at (silent **g**)
> trick: The **gn**arled **gn**ome **gn**ashed his teeth as he **gn**awed a **gn**at.

awed: cut, bit, and wore away with the teeth
> trouble spot: **gn**awed (silent **g**)
> trick: The **gn**arled **gn**ome **gn**ashed his teeth as he **gn**awed a **gn**at.

gnome: a dwarf
> trouble spot: **gn**ome (silent **g**)
> trick: The **gn**arled **gn**ome **gn**ashed his teeth as he **gn**awed a **gn**at.

government: system for maintaining order in a society
    trouble spot: go**vern**ment
    trick: A **govern**ment **govern**s **over** the society.

governor: chief administrative officer of a state government
    trouble spot: govern**or**
    trick: Neither the senat**or nor** the gover**nor** voted.

graham: kind c⸳   ur
    trouʰˡ⸱   raham
    tⁿⁱᶜ   e **ham** on my gra**ham** cracker.

grammar: rules for how a language works
    trouble spot: gra**mmar**
    trick: **Gramma** sure knows her **grammar**.

grateful: thankful
    trouble spot: gr**ate**ful (one **l**)
    trick: Be gr**ate**ful we don't h**ate bul**bs.

gravel: mixture of pebbles and cement
    trouble spot: grav**el**
    trick: Put some **gravel** on my **grave**.

grieve: sorrow for
    trouble spot: gr**ie**ve
    trick: **I** gr**ie**ve for **Eve**.

grievous: deplorable
    trou ˙ spot: grie**vous** (no **i** between **v** and **o**)
    trick: It's gr**ievous** to **vou**ch for a misch**ievous** kid.

grocery: food store
    trouble spot: gro**c**ery
    trick: I'm using the gro**c**ery **c**art.

guarantee: assure the quality
    trouble spot: g**uar**antee
    trick: This **guar**antee **guar**ds you for free.

guitar: stringed musical instrument
    trouble spot: g**ui**tar
    trick: I wear a s**ui**t when I play g**ui**tar.

handful: small amount
  trouble spot: handful (one **l**)
  trick: I bought a hand**ful** of bu**l**bs.

handsome: good-looking
  trouble spot: han**d**some
  trick: You have **hands**ome **hands**.

hangar: storage place for an airplane
  trouble spot: hang**ar** (not *hanger*)
  trick: A han**gar** is a **gar**age for planes.

hanger: device for hanging clothes
  trouble spot: hang**er** (not *hangar*)
  trick: I feel **anger** when clothes aren't on h**anger**s.

happened: occurred
  trouble spot: ha**pp**ened
  trick: I'm **happy** it **happ**ened.

harass: bother
  trouble spot: ha**r**ass (one **r**)
  trick: **Ha,** how c**rass** to **harass**!

hardware: equipment
  trouble spot: hard**ware**
  trick: Military hard**ware** is for **war**.

having: possessing
    trouble spot: ha**vi**ng (no **e** between **v** and **i**)
    trick: You can't have an **e** in **having**.

Hawaii: U.S. state
    trouble spot: Hawa**ii**
    trick: Hawa**ii** is **i**sland after **i**sland.

hazard: danger
    trouble spot: ha**z**ard (one **z**)
    trick: **Z**ap the ha**z**ard in the yard.

heaven: dwelling place of God
    trouble spot: h**ea**ven
    trick: When do you l**ea**ve for h**ea**ven?

height: topmost point
    trouble spot: h**ei**ght
    trick: N**ei**ther l**ei**sured for**ei**gn counterf**ei**ter could s**ei**ze **ei**ther w**ei**rd h**ei**ght without forf**ei**ting prot**ei**n.

heroes: plural of hero
    trouble spot: her**oes**
    trick: There were her**oes** facing torped**oes** while eating tomat**oes** and potat**oes**.

hideous: horrible to see
    trouble spot: hid**e**ous
    trick: **Hide** from a **hide**ous monster.

hindrance: obstacle
    trouble spot: hind**r**ance (no **e** between **d** and **r**)
    trick: **Drat**, all the frag**r**ances at the ent**rance** are a hind**rance**.

hippopotamus: large animal
    trouble spot: hippop**ot**amus
    trick: Fill the hippo**potamus pot** for **us**.

hoard: hide supplies
    trouble spot: h**oa**rd (not *horde*)
    trick: Don't h**oard** the **oar**s.

There were heroes facing torpedoes while
eating tomatoes and potatoes.

hoarse: having a harsh or grating sound
    trouble spot: h**oar**se (not *horse*)
    trick: I **roar**ed myself h**oar**se.

holiday: special day
    trouble spot: holiday
    trick: Put a **lid** on ho**lid**ay celebrating.

hoping: desiring
    trouble spot: ho**pi**ng (no **e** between **p** and **i**; not *hopping*)
    trick: I'm ho**pin**g the **pin** won't stick me.

horde: wandering tribe; large, moving crowd
    trouble spot: h**orde** (not *hoard*)
    trick: **Order** the h**orde** to move.

hosiery: stockings
    trouble spot: hos**iery**
    trick: I like **fiery** hos**iery**.

hostile: not hospitable
    trouble spot: host**ile**
    trick: The **Nile** River is host**ile**.

Hungary: European country
 trouble spot: Hung**ar**y (not *hungry*)
 trick: **Hungar**y is the home of **Hungar**ians.

hungry: wanting food
 trouble spot: hun**gry** (not *Hungary*)
 trick: Your stomach **gr**owls when **y**ou're hun**gry**.

hypocrisy: pretense
 trouble spot: hypocrisy
 trick: Hypo**cri**sy is **ris**ky.

ignorant: uninformed
 trouble spot: ignorant
 trick: Igno**rant** people **rant**.

illumination: light
 trouble spot: i**ll**umination
 trick: Neon **ill**umination makes me **ill**.

imitate: copy
 trouble spot: i**m**itate (one **m**)
 trick: **Limit** what you **imit**ate.

immediately: right away
    trouble spot: im**m**edi**ate**ly
    trick: We **ate** our **m**&**m**'s® immediately.

immigrant: person who moves into a country
    trouble spot: i**mm**igrant
    trick: **Imm**igrants came to **M**aine and **M**innesota.

impossible: not possible
    trouble spot: impo**ss**i**b**le
    trick: It's impo**ss**ible to mi**ss** with the **B**ible.

incidentally: by the way
    trouble spot: incident**all**y
    trick: Incident**ally,** where's **S**ally?

independent: self-reliant
    trouble spot: indepen**dent**
    trick: The indepen**dent** voters didn't make a **dent** in the election.

indispensable: absolutely necessary
    trouble spot: indi**s**pens**able**
    trick: If she **is able,** she's indi**spensable**.

industrial: relating to industry
    trouble spot: indus**trial**
    trick: Watch the **trial** of the indus**trial** polluters.

inevitable: unavoidable
    trouble spot: inevi**table**
    trick: The collapse of the **table** was inevi**table**.

inflammable: easily set on fire
    trouble spot: infla**mm**able
    trick: Trees are more infla**mm**able in su**mm**er.

ingenious: clever
    trouble spot: ingen**iou**s
    trick: **I o** (owe) **u** (you) an ingen**iou**s explanation.

Trees are more inflammable in summer.

innocent: not guilty
    trouble spot: in**n**ocent
    trick: **In no cent**ury is murder an **innocent** crime.

inoculation: injection
    trouble spot: i**n**oculation (one **n**)
    trick: An **in**oculation is an **in**jection.

insistent: demanding
    trouble spot: insis**t**ent
    trick: Sis was insis**tent** about the **tent**.

instead: in place of
    trouble spot: inst**ea**d
    trick: Drink **tea** ins**tea**d of coffee.

instructor: teacher
    trouble spot: instruct**o**r
    trick: The drill instruct**or** gave an **or**der.

intellectual: highly intelligent person
    trouble spot: inte**ll**ectual
    trick: You can't **tell** an in**tell**ectual anything.

intelligent: smart
>   trouble spot: intel**li**gent
>   trick: A p**ig** is an intel**lig**ent animal.

interesting: fascinating
>   trouble spot: interesting (often pronounced "in–tres–ting")
>   trick: **Inter**view someone **inter**esting.

interfere: intervene
>   trouble spot: interf**ere**
>   trick: Don't interf**ere here**.

interrupt: break into
>   trouble spot: inte**rr**upt
>   trick: To **err** is human; so is to inte**rr**upt.

irresistible: very attractive
>   trouble spot: irresist**i**ble
>   trick: Your new l**i**pstick makes you irresist**i**ble.

its: possessive pronoun of *it*
>   trouble spot: **its** (not *it's*)
>   trick: The dog **fits its** house.

it's: contraction of *it is*
>   trouble spot: i**t's** (not *its*)
>   trick: Check **it's** by substituting **it is** to see if the sentence still makes sense.

jeopardize: put into danger
>   trouble spot: j**eo**pardize
>   trick: Pronounce *jeopardize* "je–o–par–dize."

judgment: decision
>   trouble spot: jud**gm**ent (also *judgement*)
>   trick: Use your own **judgment**, an **e** or not.

kerosene: thin oil used as fuel
　　trouble spot: ker**ose**ne
　　trick: The **o**il in ker**ose**ne has **ene**rgy.

kindergarten: school for young children
　　trouble spot: kindergarten
　　trick: Teach **art** in kinderg**art**en.

knowledge: information
　　trouble spot: knowle**dge**
　　trick: Knowl**edge** gives you the **edge**.

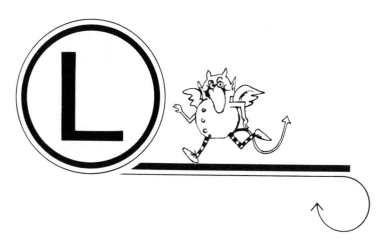

laid: past tense of *lay*
    trouble spot: l**aid**
    trick: Did the hen get p**aid** for the egg it l**aid**?

language: symbolic communication
    trouble spot: lang**ua**ge
    trick: Pronounce *language* "lan–gu–age."

later: after
    trouble spot: la**t**er (one **t**; not *latter*)
    trick: I **ate** la**t**er than you.

latitude: a measure of north and south on the globe and earth
    trouble spot: la**tit**ude
    trick: You know you're **at it** if you have the right la**tit**ude.

latter: second of two things
    trouble spot: la**tt**er (not *later*)
    trick: The la**tter** ba**tter** is the be**tter** ba**tter**.

lawyer: attorney
    trouble spot: lawyer
    trick: **Law ye**s, **lawye**rs no.

No brats in the library.

league: association
    trouble spot: lea**gue**
    trick: In this lea**gue** it doesn't pay to ar**gue**.

led: guide; past tense of *lead*
    trouble spot: l**e**d (not *lead*)
    trick: I l**e**d him to b**e**d.

leisured: having free time
    trouble spot: l**ei**sured
    trick: N**ei**ther l**ei**sured for**ei**gn counterf**ei**ter could s**ei**ze **ei**ther w**ei**rd h**ei**ght without forf**ei**ting prot**ei**n.

liable: likely
    trouble spot: l**ia**ble
    trick: A **lia**r is **lia**ble to cause trouble.

liaison: connection
    trouble spot: l**iai**son
    trick: Pronounce *liaison* "li–a–i–son."

library: place where books are stored and circulated
    trouble spot: lib**r**ary
    trick: No **bra**ts in the lib**ra**ry!

license: permission given by law
    trouble spot: li**c**e**n**se
    trick: They don't **licen**se **lice pens**.

lieutenant: officer
    trouble spot: **lieu**tenant
    trick: Don't **lie u** (you) **lieu**tenant.

lightning: electrical flash in the sky
    trouble spot: ligh**tn**ing (no **e** between **t** and **n**)
    trick: Ligh**tn**ing struck the **e** from ligh**tn**ing.

literature: compositions
    trouble spot: lit**era**ture
    trick: What's the lit**era**ture of this **era**?

livelihood: means of living
    trouble spot: liv**e**lihood
    trick: To stay a**live**, you need a **live**lihood.

loneliness: feeling alone
    trouble spot: l**one**liness
    trick: **One** a**lone** may feel **lone**liness.

loose: not tight
    trouble spot: lo**o**se (not *lose*)
    trick: What would a **loose goose** ch**oose**?

lose: misplace
    trouble spot: lose (one **o**; not *loose*)
    trick: It's hard to l**ose** your n**ose**.

losing: misplacing
    trouble spot: l**o**sing (one **o**; no **e** between **s** and **i**)
    trick: You'll keep **losing** customers if you **sing** at c**losing** time.

luggage: baggage
    trouble spot: lu**gg**age
    trick: **G**et a **g**ood **g**rip on your lu**gg**age.

magnificent: wonderful
    trouble spot: magnifi**c**ent
    trick: The **ice** may be magnif**icent**, but it isn't worth a **cent**.

maintain: keep up
    trouble spot: m**ain**tain
    trick: Even when it **rain**s and **rain**s, we must m**ain**tain the roads.

maintenance: upkeep
    trouble spot: maint**en**ance (contrast with *maintain*)
    trick: Main**ten**ance stops at **ten** P.M.

manageable: controllable
    trouble spot: manag**e**able
    trick: When you're **able** to **manage** something, it's **manageable**.

management: administration
    trouble spot: man**age**ment
    trick: This is the **age** of man**age**ment.

mantel: shelf above a fireplace
    trouble spot: mant**el**
    trick: The **elf** sits on the mant**el**.

manufacture: produce
> trouble spot: man**u**facture
> trick: Can we **manu**facture it using **manu**al labor?

marriage: wedlock
> trouble spot: marr**i**age
> trick: **I** must be in my marr**i**age.

marshmallow: kind of confection
> trouble spot: marshm**all**ow
> trick: Marshm**all**ows are **all** sugar.

mathematics: study and use of numbers and symbols
> trouble spot: mat**hem**atics
> trick: Teach **them** mat**hem**atics.

maybe: perhaps
> trouble spot: ma**ybe** (often misspelled *mabye*)
> trick: **Maybe** is a compound of **may** and **be**.

meanness: bad temper
> trouble spot: mea**nn**ess
> trick: (*Ness*-Enders, page 61)

meant: past tense of *mean*
> trouble spot: m**ean**t
> trick: He **mean**t to be **mean**.

medicine: healing arts
> trouble spot: medi**cine**
> trick: A **medic** practices **medicine** to keep you feeling **fine**.

medieval: of the middle ages
> trouble spot: me**die**val
> trick: Knights **die**d **val**iantly in me**dieval** times.

menace: threaten
> trouble spot: men**ace**
> trick: The men men**ace** us with their f**ace**s.

The men menace us with their faces.

mention: refer to
    trouble spot: men**tion**
    trick: Please m**ention** my inv**ention**.

merchandise: goods for sale
    trouble spot: merchand**ise**
    trick: Is it **wise** to buy used merchand**ise**?

merely: simply
    trouble spot: me**rely**
    trick: **Me rely** on you, is that **merely** what you want?

mileage: distance in miles
    trouble spot: mil**e**age
    trick: There's a full **mile** in **mile**age.

minimum: least amount
    trouble spot: min**i**mum
    trick: We bought the **mini**car for the **mini**mum cost.

miscellaneous: mixed together
    trouble spot: mi**scell**aneous
    trick: **Science** deals with mi**scell**aneous **cell**s.

mischievous: troublesome
  trouble spot: mischie**vo**us (no **i** between **v** and **o**)
  trick: It's grie**vous** to **vou**ch for a mischie**vous** kid.

missile: something thrown or shot
  trouble spot: m**issile**
  trick: A **missile** shouldn't **miss** by a m**ile**.

Missouri: U.S. state
  trouble spot: Mi**ssour**i
  trick: We'll always **miss our Missour**i.

misspell: spell incorrectly
  trouble spot: mi**ss**pell
  trick: **Miss Pell** can't spell **misspell**.

moccasins: kind of Indian shoe
  trouble spot: mo**cc**asins
  trick: Do **c**amp **c**ounselors **sin** in mo**cca**sins?

model: person who shows off clothing
  trouble spot: mod**el**
  trick: I'd love to hear that mo**del** yo**del** in the mot**el**.

moisten: make wet
  trouble spot: moisten (silent **t**)
  trick: Mois**ten ten** towels.

monotonous: boring
  trouble spot: m**o**n**o**t**o**n**o**us
  trick: Four **o**'s in m**o**n**o**t**o**n**o**us are m**o**n**o**t**o**n**o**us to **us.**

morale: spirit
  trouble spot: moral**e** (silent **e**; not *moral*)
  trick: Give them **ale** to boost their mor**ale**.

mortgage: pledge of property as security for a loan
  trouble spot: mor**t**gage (silent **t**)
  trick: Pronounce *mortgage* "mort–gage."

mourning: expressing grief
  trouble spot: m**our**ning (not *morning*)
  trick: We are m**our**ning **our** loss.

movable: capable of changing positions
    trouble spot: mo**va**ble (also spelled *moveable*)
    trick: You can move the **e** in or out of **movable**.

municipal: relating to a city
    trouble spot: munici**pal**
    trick: I have a **pal** on the munici**pal** council.

murmur: make low sounds
    trouble spot: mu**r**mu**r**
    trick: "**Mur**der, **mur**der," **murmur**s the crowd.

muscle: type of body tissue
    trouble spot: mus**c**le
    trick: If you have **musc**les, you're **musc**ular.

museum: place where artifacts are displayed
    trouble spot: mus**e**um
    trick: **Use** the mus**e**um.

mustache: hair on the upper lip
    trouble spot: musta**che**
    trick: Who said a **mustache must ache**?

mysterious: unknown
    trouble spot: myster**iou**s
    trick: **My**, isn't it **myster**iou**s** how **I o** (owe) **u** (you) more money?

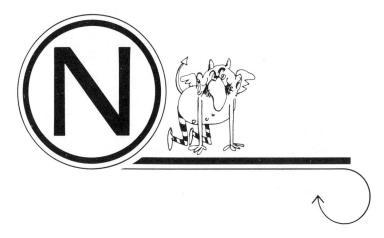

naive: unsophisticated
    trouble spot: n**ai**ve
    trick: M**a**, **I've** been n**ai**ve.

naturally: as one might expect
    trouble spot: natur**all**y
    trick: Natu**rally**, we're going to the **rally**.

necessary: needed
    trouble spot: ne**c**e**ss**ary
    trick: Is **recess** ne**cess**ary?

necessity: requirement
    trouble spot: ne**c**e**ss**ity
    trick: It's a p**ity** that **recess** is a ne**cessity**.

neighbor: person living nearby
    trouble spot: n**ei**ghbor
    trick: Our n**ei**ghbor's **eig**ht b**ei**ge r**ei**ndeer w**ei**ghed too
    much to send by fr**ei**ght.

neither: not either
    trouble spot: n**ei**ther
    trick: N**ei**ther l**ei**sured for**ei**gn counterf**ei**ter could s**ei**ze
    either w**ei**rd h**ei**ght without forf**ei**ting prot**ei**n.

niece: daughter of one's sibling
　　trouble spot: ni**e**ce
　　trick: My ni**e**ce gave me a pi**e**ce of pi**e**.

nineteen: ten plus nine
　　trouble spot: nin**e**teen
　　trick: **Nine teen**s *are* **nineteen**.

ninety: ten times nine
　　trouble spot: nin**e**ty
　　trick: **Nine ty**pewriters typed **ninety** times.

ninth: one more than *eighth*
　　trouble spot: ni**nth** (no **e** between **n** and **t**)
　　trick: The ni**nth** mo**nth** is September.

noticeable: conspicuous
　　trouble spot: notic**e**able
　　trick: You should be **able** to **notice** the **e** in **noticeable**.

nuisance: bother
　　trouble spot: n**ui**sance
　　trick: **U** (you) **is** a n**ui**sance.

obliged: indebted
   trouble spot: obli**g**ed
   trick: An **oblig**ation makes you feel **oblig**ed.

oboe: musical instrument
   trouble spot: ob**oe**
   trick: Can you play an ob**oe** with your t**oe**?

observant: watchful
   trouble spot: observ**a**nt
   trick: An **observant servant** has kept the **ant**s under **observa**tion.

obstacle: barrier
   trouble spot: obsta**cle**
   trick: The obsta**cle** knocked me **cle**ar off my bicy**cle**.

occasion: event
   trouble spot: o**cc**asion (one **s**)
   trick: Eat **c**andy and **c**ookies on special o**cc**asions.

occasionally: now and then
   trouble spot: occasiona**ll**y
   trick: We **all** fail occasion**all**y.

occur: happen
   trouble spot: o**cc**ur (one **r**)
   trick: What might o**cc**ur on a **c**able **c**ar **r**ide?

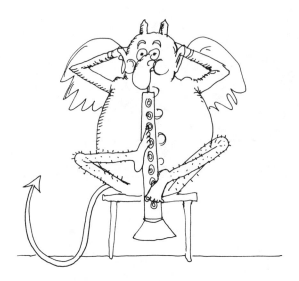

Can you play an oboe with your toe?

occurred: happened
> trouble spot: o**cc**u**rr**ed
> trick: The **c**able **c**ar wreck o**cc**u**rr**ed in a hu**rr**y.

occurrence: happening
> trouble spot: o**cc**u**rr**ence
> trick: Was the **c**able **c**ar a**cc**ident a **r**ather **r**e**c**ent o**cc**u**rr**ence?

often: frequently
> trouble spot: of**t**en (**t** is usually silent)
> trick: Nine out **of ten** times is **often** enough.

omitted: left out
> trouble spot: o**m**itted (one **m**)
> trick: The coach o**mitt**ed the **mitt** from our equipment list.

only: alone of its kind
> trouble spot: o**nl**y (sometimes misspelled *olny*)
> trick: I was the **only onl**ooker.

opinion: belief
>trouble spot: opinion (one **p**; one **n**)
>trick: I wouldn't give a **pin** for your o**pin**ion about **ion**s.

opponent: adversary
>trouble spot: o**pp**onent
>trick: Who wants a hi**ppo** for an o**pp**onent in a **tent**?

opportunity: good chance
>trouble spot: o**pp**ortunity
>trick: Be ha**pp**y when an o**pp**ortunity ha**pp**ens.

opposite: as different as possible; across
>trouble spot: o**pposite**
>trick: The hi**ppo** lives on the **site** o**pposite** my house.

optimistic: hopeful
>trouble spot: op**tim**istic
>trick: **Tim** is always op**tim**istic.

orangutan: type of ape
>trouble spot: orang**utan** (**n** is the last letter)
>trick: Will **u** (you) **tan**, orang**utan**?

outrageous: terrible
>trouble spot: out**rage**ous
>trick: This is the **age** of out**rage**ous clothes.

overrate: value too highly
>trouble spot: ove**rr**ate
>trick: It's an **err**or to ove**rr**ate.

overrule: annul
>trouble spot: ove**rr**ule
>trick: It's an **err**or to ove**rr**ule the majority.

pageant: spectacle
trouble spot: pag**e**ant
trick: Write a **page** about the **ant pageant**.

paid: past tense of *pay*
trouble spot: pa**i**d
trick: I p**aid** for first **aid**.

pajamas: loose garment worn to bed
trouble spot: paja**m**as (one **m**)
trick: **Pa** and **ma** wear **pa**ja**ma**s.

pale: colorless
trouble spot: pa**le** (not *pail*)
trick: A glass of **ale** made my **pal pale**.

pamphlet: small booklet
trouble spot: pam**ph**let
trick: **Pam ph**oned for the **pamph**let.

pane: piece or sheet of glass
trouble spot: pa**ne** (not *pain*)
trick: A **pane** of glass is a **pane**l.

panicky: fearful
trouble spot: pani**ck**y
trick: Being s**ick** makes me pan**ick**y.

parallel: side by side
    trouble spot: para**ll**el
    trick: **All l**ines are not para**ll**el.

paralysis: inability to function
    trouble spot: paral**ysis**
    trick: **Y** (why) does **sis** have paral**ysis**?

paralyze: take away the ability to move
    trouble spot: paral**yze**
    trick: **Y** (why) paral**yze** a **ze**bra?

parliament: assembly for making laws
    trouble spot: parl**iam**ent
    trick: **I am** in the parl**iam**ent.

partial: not complete
    trouble spot: par**t**ial
    trick: **Part**ial means **part** of something.

passed: past tense of *pass*
    trouble spot: pa**ss**ed (not *past*)
    trick: The **ass** pa**ss**ed me by.

past: by
    trouble spot: p**ast** (not *passed*)
    trick: I went p**ast** your house l**ast** week.

past: former time
    trouble spot: p**ast** (not *passed*)
    trick: L**ast** year is in the p**ast**.

pastime: amusement
    trouble spot: pastime (one **s**; one **t**)
    trick: My **pastime**s change **as time** goes by.

patience: endurance
    trouble spot: pa**tie**nce
    trick: It takes pa**tie**nce to **tie** a bow**tie**.

pavilion: exhibition area
    trouble spot: pavi**l**ion (one **l**)
    trick: The **lion** is in the cat pavi**lion**.

peace: quiet
> trouble spot: p**eace** (not *piece*)
> trick: The s**ea** is full of p**eace**.

peaceable: not quarrelsome
> trouble spot: peac**e**able
> trick: **Able** to keep the **peace** means **peaceable**.

peculiar: strange
> trouble spot: pecu**liar**
> trick: A **liar** is a pecu**liar** person.

penicillin: antibiotic drug
> trouble spot: penici**ll**in
> trick: When **ill**, take penc**ill**in.

peninsula: land surrounded on three sides by water
> trouble spot: p**en**insula (one **n**)
> trick: I lost my **pen** on the **pen**insula.

performance: doing of a task
> trouble spot: perfor**m**a**n**ce
> trick: The **man** da**n**ced a great perfor**man**ce.

permanent: lasting
> trouble spot: per**man**ent
> trick: Is your **mane** per**man**ent?

permissible: allowed
> trouble spot: permi**ss**ible
> trick: Is it per**missible** to **miss Bible** class?

perseverant: tenacious
> trouble spot: pers**ev**erant (no **r** between **e** and **v**)
> trick: The **ant** is **ever** pers**ever**ant.

persevere: stay with a task
> trouble spot: persev**ere**
> trick: Everyone **here** should persev**ere**.

persistent: determined
> trouble spot: per**sistent**
> trick: **Sis** was per**sistent** about raising the **tent**.

Is your mane permanent?

personal: private
> trouble spot: person**al** (not *personnel*)
> trick: You're my person**al** **pal**.

personally: in one's own opinion
> trouble spot: person**ally**
> trick: Person**ally**, I like S**ally**.

personnel: people working on a job
> trouble spot: perso**nnel** (not *personal*)
> trick: We have some fu**nny** perso**nnel** working in the tu**nnel**.

perspiration: sweat
> trouble spot: per**spir**ation
> trick: When you **perspire**, you have **perspir**ation.

persuade: convince
> trouble spot: pers**ua**de
> trick: Pronounce *persuade* "per–su–ade."

Are there pillars on Mars?

petal: flower part
> trouble spot: petal (not *pedal* or *peddle*)
> trick: My **pet** snail ate a **pet**al.

physician: doctor
> trouble spot: **phy**sician
> trick: **Y** (why) **ph**one the **phy**sician?

physique: structure of one's body
> trouble spot: ph**ysique**
> trick: **Y** (why) **que**stion my ph**ysique**?

piccolo: musical instrument resembling the flute but smaller
> trouble spot: pi**cc**olo
> trick: The pi**cc**olo plays from low **c** to high **c**.

picnicking: holding a picnic
> trouble spot: picnic**k**ing
> trick: Who's the **king** of picnic**king**?

piece: part of something
> trouble spot: pi**ece** (not *peace*)
> trick: I want a **pie**ce of **pie**.

pigeon: kind of bird
> trouble spot: pigeon (no **d** between **i** and **g**)
> trick: The **pig** and **pig**eon have been here for **eons**.

pillar: column
>   trouble spot: pillar
>   trick: Are there pill**ars** on **Mars**?

pincers: a gripping tool
>   trouble spot: pincers
>   trick: Did you **wince** when the **prince** used **pincers**?

pistil: flower part
>   trouble spot: pistil (not *pistol*)
>   trick: Wait unt**il** the pist**il** w**il**ts.

pistol: small gun
>   trouble spot: pistol (not *pistil*)
>   trick: I sh**ot** with my pist**ol**.

Pittsburgh: U.S. city in Pennsylvania
>   trouble spot: Pittsburg**h** (silent **h**)
>   trick: Pittsburg**h** and **H**ershey are both in Pennsylvania.

plague: contagious epidemic disease
>   trouble spot: plag**ue**
>   trick: A plag**ue** of gl**ue** on you!

plaid: pattern of stripes crossing at right angles
>   trouble spot: pl**ai**d
>   trick: We **laid** out the pl**ai**d pattern.

plane: short for airplane
>   trouble spot: pl**ane** (not *plain*)
>   trick: You need a **plan** to fly a **plane**.

planned: arranged
>   trouble spot: pla**nn**ed
>   trick: **Ann** pla**nn**ed.

planning: preparing
>   trouble spot: pla**nn**ing
>   trick: **Ann** is pla**nn**ing a trip.

playwright: a dramatist
>   trouble spot: play**wright**
>   trick: The play**wright** **wr**ote **right**-handed.

pleasant: agreeable
> trouble spot: pl**ea**sant
> trick: The **east** coast is pl**ea**sant.

politician: person engaged in politics
> trouble spot: poli**ti**cian
> trick: **Politic**ians must be **polit**e to do well in **politic**s.

pomegranate: a fruit
> trouble spot: pom**e**gran**ate**
> trick: At h**ome** I **ate** a p**ome**gran**ate**.

porcelain: kind of ceramic
> trouble spot: porcel**ain**
> trick: The porcel**ain** container has **lain** here all night.

porpoise: dolphin
> trouble spot: porp**oise**
> trick: A porp**oise** makes an interesting n**oise**.

possess: own
> trouble spot: po**ssess**
> trick: No one can po**ssess** the Mississippi.

possible: capable of being done
> trouble spot: pos**sib**le
> trick: It's pos**sib**le I'm mis**sib**... my **Bib**le.

potatoes: kind of vegetable
> trouble spot: potat**oes**
> trick: There were her**oes** facing torped**oes** while eating
> tomat**oes** and potat**oes**.

practically: almost
> trouble spot: practic**ally**
> trick: S**ally** practic**ally** broke her neck.

practice: repeated effort
> trouble spot: pract**ice**
> trick: Pract**ice** driving on **ice**.

Practice driving on ice.

prairie: a large area of grassland
> trouble spot: pr**air**ie
> trick: There's good **air** on the prairie.

preceded: go before
> trouble spot: pre**ceded**
> trick: He pre**ced**ed me; he **c**ame **e**arlier and **d**ied **e**arlier.

preceding: before
> trouble spot: preceding (one **e**)
> trick: **Prece**ding the **rece**ption, pictures will be taken.

precious: of great value
> trouble spot: preci**ou**s
> trick: **I o** (owe) **u** (you) a preci**ou**s gem.

precocious: advanced
> trouble spot: pre**co**c**io**us
> trick: The pre**co**cious child loves **co**coa.

prefer: favor
> trouble spot: prefer (one **f**)
> trick: I pre**fer** a **fer**n.

prejudice: bias
> trouble spot: prejudice (no **d** between **e** and **j**)
> trick: When you **prejudg**e, you have a **prejud**ice.

preparation: readiness
> trouble spot: prep**a**ration
> trick: **Pa** taught us prep**a**ration.

prevalent: widely existing or practiced
> trouble spot: preval**e**nt
> trick: **Ale** is the preval**e**nt beverage around here.

prey: hunt for food
> trouble spot: pr**e**y (not *pray*)
> trick: A **pre**ditor **pre**ys.

principal: head of a school
> trouble spot: princi**pal** (not *principle*)
> trick: The school princi**pal** is your **pal**.

principle: rule
> trouble spot: princi**ple** (not *principal*)
> trick: The princi**ple** that serves as a guideline is a ru**le**.

privilege: advantage
> trouble spot: pri**vile**ge
> trick: It's **vile** that the rich have pri**vile**ges.

probably: more likely than not
> trouble spot: prob**a**bly
> trick: The **bab**y prob**ab**ly did it.

procedure: method
> trouble spot: proc**e**dure (one **e**)
> trick: **Ed** taught me the proc**ed**ure.

proceed: continue
> trouble spot: proc**ee**d
> trick: Proc**eed** at full sp**eed**.

prodigy: person with extraordinary ability
> trouble spot: pro**di**gy
> trick: The pro**digy** **dig**s into books.

professor: college teacher
> trouble spot: profe**ss**o**r**
> trick: Con**fess or** else, pro**fessor**.

prominent: well known
    trouble spot: pro**min**ent
    trick: This pro**min**ent leader is a friend of **mine**.

pronounce: speak aloud
    trouble spot: pron**oun**ce
    trick: Pro**noun**ce the **noun**.

pronunciation: way of saying words
    trouble spot: pro**nun**ciation
    trick: The **nun** has good pro**nun**ciation.

propaganda: information intended to convince
    trouble spot: prop**agan**da
    trick: This is **pagan** prop**agan**da.

propagate: to breed
    trouble spot: prop**a**gate
    trick: **Pa** told us to prop**a**gate.

propeller: a device with blades used for propulsion
    trouble spot: propell**er**
    trick: I'm a propell**er** sell**er**.

prophecy: prediction
    trouble spot: prophe**cy** (not *prophesy*)
    trick: Nan**cy** made a prophe**cy**.

prophesy: predict
    trouble spot: prophe**sy** (not *prophecy*)
    trick: It takes **ski**ll to prophe**sy**.

protein: cellular building material
    trouble spot: prot**ei**n
    trick: **N**either l**ei**sured for**ei**gn counterf**ei**ter could s**ei**ze **ei**ther w**ei**rd h**ei**ght without forf**ei**ting prot**ei**n.

psychology: science of behavior
    trouble spot: **ps**ychology
    trick: **P.S. Y** (why) are you studying **ps**ychology?

purchase: buy
    trouble spot: purchase
    trick: **Pur**chase the **pur**se.

pursue: go after
    trouble spot: pursue
    trick: **Purs**ue a lost **purs**e.

quantity: an amount
    trouble spot: quantity
    trick: There's a large quan**tity** of garbage in the **city**.

questionnaire: survey form
    trouble spot: questio**nn**aire
    trick: The questio**nn**aire at the **inn** raised my **ire**.

quiet: stillness
    trouble spot: qu**iet** (not *quite*)
    trick: I ate a qu**iet** d**iet** of soup and bread.

quite: very
    trouble spot: qu**ite** (not *quiet*)
    trick: I took qu**ite** a **bite**.

raccoon: masked mammal
>trouble spot: ra**cc**oo**n**
>trick: A ra**cc**oo**n** is twice the bother (**cc, oo**) of other animals.

ransom: pay money to free a hostage
>trouble spot: ranso**m** (no **e** at the end)
>trick: Rans**om T**om.

rapport: harmony
>trouble spot: rappor**t** (silent **t**)
>trick: Our ha**pp**y **rapport** needs your su**pport**.

raspberry: kind of fruit
>trouble spot: ras**p**berry (silent **p**)
>trick: I **grasp** the **rasp**berry.

realize: understand
>trouble spot: re**a**lize
>trick: **Real**ity's s**ize** is hard to **realize**.

really: truly
>trouble spot: re**all**y
>trick: Are you re**all**y Sa**ll**y?

receipt: proof of purchase
　　trouble spot: recei**p**t (silent **p**)
　　trick: He's a**pt** to forget the **p** in recei**pt**.

receivable: due
　　trouble spot: recei**va**ble (no **e** between **v** and **a**)
　　trick: The **valuable**s are recei**vable**.

receive: to get
　　trouble spot: rec**ei**ve
　　trick: (*I Before E*, page 120)

recipe: procedure for cooking
　　trouble spot: rec**ipe**
　　trick: The rec**ipe** says to **wipe** the **ripe** fruit.

reckless: careless
　　trouble spot: **r**eckless (no **w**)
　　trick: **R**ick is **r**eckless.

recognize: know someone or something
　　trouble spot: reco**g**nize
　　trick: Can you reco**g**nize your **dog**?

recommend: suggest
　　trouble spot: re**c**o**mm**end
　　trick: What re**c**ords do you re**comm**end for su**mm**er?

recruit: new member
　　trouble spot: recr**uit**
　　trick: The new recr**uit** wears a s**uit**.

refer: send
　　trouble spot: re**f**er (one **f**)
　　trick: **Ref**er the quarterback to the **ref**.

referred: mentioned
　　trouble spot: refe**rr**ed
　　trick: He was refe**rr**ed in **err**or.

regrettable: unfortunate
　　trouble spot: regre**tt**able
　　trick: How **regrettable** to **regret table**s.

I grasp the raspberry.

rehearse: practice
>trouble spot: reh**ear**se
>trick: **Hear** the band re**hear**se.

reindeer: hooved mammals
>trouble spot: r**ei**ndeer
>trick: Our n**ei**ghbor's **ei**ght b**ei**ge r**ei**ndeer w**ei**ghed too much to send by fr**ei**ght.

relevant: pertinent
>trouble spot: relev**ant**
>trick: A picnic's relev**ant** to **ant**s.

relief: help
>trouble spot: rel**ie**f
>trick: A **lie** offers no rel**ie**f.

religious: devout
>trouble spot: relig**iou**s
>trick: Do **I o** (owe) **u** (you) a relig**iou**s experience?

remembrance: recollection
>trouble spot: remem**br**ance (no **e** between **b** and **r**)
>trick: The tree had a remem**branc**e of **branc**hes past.

rendezvous: place set for a meeting
 trouble spot: rendezvou**s**
 trick: Pronounce *rendezvous* "ren–dez–vous."

renown: great fame
 trouble spot: re**now**n (no **k**)
 trick: **Now** she has **renow**n in **Reno**.

repentant: sorry
 trouble spot: repentant
 trick: The **ant** is repen**t**ant.

repetition: repeating
 trouble spot: repetition
 trick: My **pet** loves re**pet**ition.

representative: one who acts or speaks for others
 trouble spot: representative
 trick: A **representati**ve gives us **representati**on.

rescind: cancel
 trouble spot: rescind
 trick: **Resc**ind the **resc**ue call.

response: answer
 trouble spot: response
 trick: **S**end a respon**se** by mail.

restaurant: eating place
 trouble spot: rest**au**rant
 trick: This **restaura**nt has a **rest**ful **aura**.

rhapsody: a kind of musical composition
 trouble spot: **r**hapsody (silent **h**)
 trick: That **chap** wrote a **rhap**sody.

rhetorical: relating to the art of using words effectively
 trouble spot: **r**hetorical (silent **h**)
 trick: A **rh**eumatic **rh**inoceros practices **rh**etorical **rh**ymes while eating **rh**ododendrons and **rh**ubarb in **Rh**ode Island.

rheumatic: having pain in joints and muscles
    trouble spot: rheumatic (silent **h**)
    trick: A **rh**eumatic **rh**inoceros practices **rh**etorical **rh**ymes while eating **rh**ododendrons and **rh**ubarb in **Rh**ode Island.

rhinoceros: large animal
    trouble spot: rhinoceros (silent **h**)
    trick: A **rh**eumatic **rh**inoceros practices **rh**etorical **rh**ymes while eating **rh**ododendrons and **rh**ubarb in **Rh**ode Island.

Rhode Island: U.S. state
    trouble spot: Rhode Island (silent **h**)
    trick: A **rh**eumatic **rh**inoceros practices **rh**etorical **rh**ymes while eating **rh**ododendrons and **rh**ubarb in **Rh**ode Island.

rhubarb: plant
    trouble spot: rhubarb (silent **h**)
    trick: A **rh**eumatic **rh**inoceros practices **rh**etorical **rh**ymes while eating **rh**ododendrons and **rh**ubarb in **Rh**ode Island.

rhymes: corresponding sounds within paired words
    trouble spot: rhymes (silent **h**)
    trick: A **rh**eumatic **rh**inoceros practices **rh**etorical **rh**ymes while eating **rh**ododendrons and **rh**ubarb in **Rh**ode Island.

ridiculous: absurd
    trouble spot: ridiculous
    trick: Get **rid** of that **rid**iculous smile.

role: part in a play
    trouble spot: ro**le** (not *roll*)
    trick: I play the **role** of a m**ole** in a h**ole**.

roll: turn
    trouble spot: ro**ll** (not *role*)
    trick: **Roll** the tro**ll** off the bridge.

roommate: room sharer
>   trouble spot: roo**mm**ate
>   trick: I have a su**mm**er roo**mm**ate.

rough: coarse; difficult
>   trouble spot: r**ough**
>   trick: I th**ough**t I'd b**ough**t en**ough cough** syrup to make it thr**ough** this r**ough,** t**ough** winter.

route: course
>   trouble spot: r**ou**te (pronounced like *rout* or *root*)
>   trick: I want to take the **outer** r**ou**te.

sacrifice: to give up something
>   trouble spot: sacr**if**ice
>   trick: **If** you sacr**if**ice, I will too.

sacrilegious: violating something sacred
>   trouble spot: sacr**il**egious
>   trick: You **rile** me with your sacr**il**egious attitude.

safety: freedom from danger
>   trouble spot: saf**e**ty
>   trick: Make something **safe** by working on **safe**ty.

salad: vegetable dish
  trouble spot: salad (one **l**)
  trick: Give the **lad** a sa**lad**.

salary: payment for employment
  trouble spot: **sal**ary (not *celery*)
  trick: **Sal**ary was once a payment in **sal**t.

sandal: kind of slipper
  trouble spot: sandal
  trick: In the **sand Al** wore one **sandal**.

sandwich: bread with filling
  trouble spot: san**dw**ich (no **t** between **i** and **c**)
  trick: **Sand** doesn't make a **sandwich rich**.

sapphire: precious stone
  trouble spot: sa**pp**hire
  trick: This sa**pp**hire makes me ha**pp**y.

satellite: orbiting object
  trouble spot: sate**ll**ite
  trick: What does the sate**ll**ite **tell** us?

satisfaction: gratification
  trouble spot: satisfa**ct**ion
  trick: Satis**fact**ion is a **fact** of life.

satisfactorily: done in an acceptable fashion
  trouble spot: satisfactor**i**ly
  trick: (Y-Ender, page 123)

satisfied: pleased
  trouble spot: satis**fied**
  trick: Satis**fied**, he **died**.

scaly: covered with scales
  trouble spot: scal**y** (no **e** between **l** and **y**)
  trick: My **scalp** is **scaly**.

scandal: an embarrassing situation
  trouble spot: scand**al**
  trick: Did you hear about the **panda scandal**?

Salary was once payment in salt.

scarcity: shortage
>trouble spot: scar**c**ity
>trick: There's a housing scar**city** in this **city**.

scene: portion of film or play
>trouble spot: **sce**ne (not *seen*)
>trick: Eug**ene** is in a sc**ary** **scene**.

scenery: features of landscape
>trouble spot: sc**ener**y
>trick: The **ene**my hides in the sc**ener**y.

scent: odor
>trouble spot: **sc**ent (not *cent* or *sent*)
>trick: Does this new **sc**ent **sc**are you?

schedule: a list of times when certain events will occur
>trouble spot: **sch**e**d**ule
>trick: The **sch**e**d**ule at **sch**ool is a kind of **rule**.

scheme: plan
>trouble spot: **sch**eme
>trick: You don't need **sch**ool to know how to **sch**eme.

scissors: a cutting tool
  trouble spot: **scis**sors
  trick: Don't be **sc**ared, M**iss,** by **sciss**ors.

sculptor: artist who creates three-dimensional works
  trouble spot: sculpt**or** (contrast with *sculpture*)
  trick: I'll be a sculpt**or or** a doct**or.**

sculpture: work of art in three dimensions
  trouble spot: sculp**ture** (contrast with *sculptor*)
  trick: A sculp**ture** is a kind of pic**ture.**

secretary: office worker
  trouble spot: sec**ret**ary
  trick: A **secret**ary keeps **secret**s.

seize: take
  trouble spot: s**ei**ze (not *cease*)
  trick: **N**either l**ei**sured for**ei**gn counterf**ei**ter could s**ei**ze **ei**ther w**ei**rd h**ei**ght without forf**ei**ting prot**ei**n.

semester: school term
  trouble spot: semester
  trick: I'm taking a **sem**inar **se**cond **sem**ester.

senator: member of senate
  trouble spot: senat**or**
  trick: The senat**or** called **for or**der.

sense: faculty of perception
  trouble spot: **sen**se (not *cents* or *scents*)
  trick: When you use your **sens**es, you get a **sens**ation.

sensible: reasonable
  trouble spot: sen**sible**
  trick: You're a sen**sible sibl**ing.

separate: move apart
  trouble spot: sep**a**r**a**te
  trick: There's **a rat** in sep**arat**e.

sergeant: noncommissioned officer
trouble spot: ser**ge**ant
trick: Pronounce *sergeant* "ser–ge–ant."

serial: story presented in separate parts
trouble spot: **seri**al (not *cereal*)
trick: A **seri**al is a **seri**es of stories.

severe: harsh
trouble spot: sev**ere**
trick: Are people sev**ere here**?

shepherd: person who tends sheep
trouble spot: shep**h**erd (silent **h**)
trick: A shep**herd herd**s sheep.

sherbet: frozen dessert
trouble spot: sherb**et** (no **r** between **e** and **t**)
trick: He took **her bet** that he couldn't spell **sherbet**.

sheriff: law officer
trouble spot: she**riff** (one **r**)
trick: A she**riff** directs t**raff**ic.

shriek: make a loud, piercing cry
trouble spot: shr**ie**k
trick: "Now you **die**!" the killer shr**ie**ked.

shrivel: wither or shrink
trouble spot: shriv**el**
trick: Shriv**el** the **el**f.

siege: strategic blockade
trouble spot: s**ie**ge
trick: Sold**ie**rs can **die** in a s**ie**ge.

similar: having a resemblance
trouble spot: s**imi**lar
trick: These two quarterbacks have s**imi**lar l**imi**tations.

sincerely: honestly
trouble spot: sincerely
trick: **Since** I **rely** on you, I **sincerely** need you.

Shrivel the elf.

skiing: winter sport
> trouble spot: sk**ii**ng
> trick: Use both **i**'s (eyes) in sk**ii**ng.

snorkel: a device for breathing under water
> trouble spot: snork**el**
> trick: My snor**kel** got caught in the **kelp**.

solder: metal alloy
> trouble spot: so**l**der (silent **l**; rhymes with *fodder*)
> trick: Who **sold** you this **sold**er?

soldier: military person
> trouble spot: sold**ier**
> trick: Old sol**diers** never **die**.

sole: bottom of foot or shoe
> trouble spot: s**ole** (not *soul*)
> trick: There's a h**ole** in the s**ole** of your shoe.

sole: one and only
> trouble spot: s**ole** (not *soul*)
> trick: That's the s**ole** m**ole** in the garden.

sole: kind of fish
>trouble spot: s**ole** (not *soul*)
>trick: I caught the s**ole** with my fishing p**ole**.

solemn: serious
>trouble spot: solem**n** (silent **n**)
>trick: When you're solem**n**, that's solem**n**ity.

somersault: acrobatic stunt
>trouble spot: s**ome**rs**ault**
>trick: **Some somer**sa**ults** have **faults**.

sometime: unspecified time
>trouble spot: **sometime** (one word)
>trick: **Sometime**, like **never**, is one word.

source: origin
>trouble spot: s**our**ce
>trick: What is the s**our**ce of this **sour** cream?

spacious: large
>trouble spot: spac**iou**s
>trick: **I o** (owe) **u** (you) a spac**iou**s place to stay.

specimen: an example or sample
>trouble spot: spe**ci**men
>trick: This **ci**gar is a spe**ci**men.

speech: talk
>trouble spot: sp**ee**ch (contrast with *speak*)
>trick: Exercise your right of fr**ee** sp**ee**ch.

sponsor: supporter
>trouble spot: spons**or**
>trick: The spons**or or**dered sh**or**t commercials.

squeak: thin, high-pitched sound
>trouble spot: squ**eak**
>trick: I sp**eak** with a squ**eak**.

squeeze: press
>trouble spot: squ**eeze**
>trick: Squ**eeze** the qu**ee**n's **ze**bra.

Squeeze the queen's zebra.

squirrel: tree-climbing rodent
    trouble spot: squi**rr**el
    trick: The squi**rr**el hu**rr**ies.

stake: pointed stick
    trouble spot: st**a**ke (not *steak*)
    trick: Turn this **rake** handle into a st**ake**.

stalactite: underground lime deposit
    trouble spot: stala**c**tite
    trick: Stala**c**tites hang from the **c**eiling.

stalagmite: underground lime deposit
    trouble spot: stala**g**mite
    trick: Stala**g**mites grow from the **g**round.

stalk: pursue
    trouble spot: sta**l**k (silent **l**)
    trick: If you don't **talk**, I'll s**talk** you.

stampede: confused mass movement
    trouble spot: stamp**ede**
    trick: The **pede**strian was hurt in the stam**pede**.

I'm crying while I'm studying.

statement: report
> trouble spot: stat**e**ment
> trick: I h**ate** the stat**e**ment.

stating: expressing
> trouble spot: sta**ti**ng (no **e** between **t** and **i**)
> trick: I'm sta**ti**ng that **tin** is valuable.

stationary: fixed in one place
> trouble spot: station**a**ry (not *stationery*)
> trick: A station**a**ry, unmoving object st**a**nds still.

stationery: paper and envelopes
> trouble spot: station**e**ry (not *stationary*)
> trick: The station**e**ry that you write letters on is pap**e**r.

steak: slice of meat
> trouble spot: st**ea**k (not *stake*)
> trick: You **ea**t a st**ea**k.

steal: take without permission
>trouble spot: st**eal** (not *steel*)
>trick: When you st**eal** a m**eal** of v**eal**, you're in r**eal** trouble.

steel: metal alloy
>trouble spot: st**eel** (not *steal*)
>trick: F**eel** the st**eel** wh**eel**.

strait: narrow waterway
>trouble spot: str**ait** (not *straight*)
>trick: We caught some b**ait** in the str**ait**.

studying: acquiring knowledge
>trouble spot: stud**y**ing
>trick: I'm cr**ying** while I'm stud**ying**.

subtle: not obvious
>trouble spot: su**b**tle (silent **b**)
>trick: Pronounce *subtle* "sub–tle."

subtly: done in a sly manner
>trouble spot: subt**ly** (no **e** between **l** and **y**)
>trick: It was done ap**tly** and sub**tly**.

succulent: juicy
>trouble spot: su**cc**u**l**ent
>trick: The **c**u**c**umber he **l**ent us was su**cc**u**l**ent.

suede: tanned leather
>trouble spot: s**ue**de
>trick: **Sue** loves s**ue**de.

sufficient: enough
>trouble spot: suffi**cient**
>trick: Is all this stuff suffi**cient** for your **client**?

suffrage: the right to vote; franchise
>trouble spot: su**ffr**age (no **e** between **f** and **r**)
>trick: The fighters for s**uffr**age didn't bl**uff rage**.

suing: seeking justice in court
  trouble spot: s**ui**ng (no **e** between **u** and **i**)
  trick: When you're s**ui**ng, you're making a s**ui**t.

suite: group of connected rooms
  trouble spot: s**uite** (not *sweet*)
  trick: I wore a new s**uit** in the wh**ite suite**.

sundae: ice cream covered with syrup
  trouble spot: sund**ae** (not *Sunday*)
  trick: I **ate** a sund**ae**.

sundries: miscellaneous things
  trouble spot: sund**ries**
  trick: The **sun dries** our **sundries**.

superintendent: person in charge
  trouble spot: superintend**ent**
  trick: Pay your **rent** to the superintend**ent**.

supersede: replace
  trouble spot: super**sede**
  trick: Super**sede** means to **set** asi**de**.

superstitious: believing in superstition
  trouble spot: super**stit**ious
  trick: The super**stit**ious seamstress will never cross her **stit**ches.

supervisor: person in charge
  trouble spot: supervis**or**
  trick: A super**visor** wears a **visor** and gives **or**ders.

supplies: provisions
  trouble spot: suppl**ies**
  trick: **Lies** are a liar's suppl**ies**.

suppress: subdue
  trouble spot: su**pp**ress
  trick: **Supp**ress your urge for **supp**er.

Urge on the surgeon.

surgeon: doctor who specializes in operations
trouble spot: su**rgeon**
trick: **Urge on** the **surgeon**.

surprise: startle
trouble spot: surpr**ise**
trick: Is it **wise** to surpr**ise** a burglar?

sweat: perspiration
trouble spot: sw**eat** (not *sweet*)
trick: The h**eat** can make you sw**eat**.

sweet: relating to one of the four sensations of taste
trouble spot: sw**eet** (not *sweat* or *suite*)
trick: A b**ee**'s honey is sw**eet**.

sword: long-bladed weapon
trouble spot: **sw**ord
trick: **Sw**ing a **sw**ord.

syllable: unit of pronunciation
trouble spot: sy**ll**able
trick: **Y** (why) a**ll** the fuss about sy**ll**ables?

symbol: something that stands for something else
trouble spot: symb**ol** (not *cymbal*)
trick: We need a **bol**d symb**ol**.

sympathy: a sharing of someone else's sorrow or trouble
 trouble spot: sym**pa**thy
 trick: **Y** (why) should I feel sym**pa**thy for you?

synagogue: a Jewish temple
 trouble spot: synagog**ue**
 trick: **Y** (why) is the synagog**ue** blue?

synonym: word with the same meaning as another word
 trouble spot: s**y**non**y**m
 trick: **Y** (why), oh **y** (why) does synonym have two **y**'s?

tail: the rear of something
 trouble spot: t**ai**l (not *tale*)
 trick: The t**ai**l of the kite will make it s**ai**l.

tailor: one who makes clothes
 trouble spot: tail**or**
 trick: **Lor**d, that tail**or** can sew!

taking: getting possession or use; indulging in
 trouble spot: ta**ki**ng (no **e** between **k** and **i**)
 trick: The **king** is ta**king** a nap.

tale: story
    trouble spot: t**ale** (not *tail*)
    trick: It takes **tale**nt to tell a **tale**.

tambourine: musical instrument
    trouble spot: tamb**our**ine
    trick: **Our** tamb**our**ine s**ou**nds fine.

tangible: having actual form
    trouble spot: tang**ible**
    trick: Are the B**ible**'s truths tang**ible**?

tariff: import tax
    trouble spot: ta**r**iff (one **r**)
    trick: The **tariff** on **tar** caused a **tiff**.

tassel: decoration
    trouble spot: tass**el**
    trick: The **el**ephant wore a tass**el**.

tattoo: skin decoration
    trouble spot: ta**ttoo**
    trick: My c**at, too**, got a **tattoo**.

tea: beverage
    trouble spot: t**ea** (not *tee*)
    trick: I like something to **ea**t with my t**ea**.

technical: relating to applied science
    trouble spot: te**ch**nical
    trick: **Ch**oose a te**ch**nical profession.

tee: a holder for a golf ball
    trouble spot: t**ee** (not *tea*)
    trick: S**ee** the golf t**ee**.

televise: to transmit by television
    trouble spot: televi**se**
    trick: Is it **wise** to televi**se**?

temperamental: unpredictable
    trouble spot: temp**era**mental
    trick: This is an **era** of temp**era**mental actors.

My cat, too, got a tattoo.

temporary: not permanent
  trouble spot: tempo**rary**
  trick: This is the **tempo**rary **tempo**.

tenant: person who rents an apartment or a house
  trouble spot: te**n**ant (one **n**)
  trick: I have **ten ants** for **tenants**.

tendency: inclination
  trouble spot: ten**den**cy
  trick: I've a ten**den**cy to hide out in my **den**.

tentacle: armlike appendage
  trouble spot: tent**a**cle
  trick: A tent**a**cle is an **arm**.

terrible: awful
  trouble spot: te**rr**ible
  trick: To **err** is not te**rr**ible, says the **Bi**ble.

testimonial: expression of gratitude
  trouble spot: tes**tim**onial
  trick: **Tim** gave me a tes**tim**onial banquet.

than: a conjunction
>trouble spot: th**an** (not *then*)
>trick: I like my **tan** more th**an** your **tan**.

their: possessive pronoun
>trouble spot: th**eir** (not *there* or *they're*)
>trick: **He** and **I** are th**ei**r sons.

then: at that time
>trouble spot: th**en** (not *than*)
>trick: **Wh**en is th**en**?

theory: explanation
>trouble spot: th**eo**ry
>trick: **Theo** has a **theo**ry.

there: at or in that place
>trouble spot: th**ere** (not *their* or *they're*)
>trick: You'll find **here** in t**here**.

therefore: so
>trouble spot: there**fore**
>trick: I'm hungry; there**fore**, I want m**ore**.

they're: contraction of *they are*
>trouble spot: the**y're** (not *their* or *there*)
>trick: Check **they're** by substituting **they are** to see if the sentence still makes sense.

thief: one who steals
>trouble spot: th**ief**
>trick: A th**ief** l**ie**s.

thoroughly: completely
>trouble spot: th**orough**ly
>trick: The Norse god **Thor** was **thorough**ly t**ough**.

thought: past tense of *think*
>trouble spot: th**ough**t
>trick: I th**ough**t I'd b**ough**t en**ough** c**ough** syrup to make it thr**ough** this r**ough**, t**ough** winter.

threw: past tense of *throw*
> trouble spot: th**r**ew (not th*rough*)
> trick: I th**r**ew the st**ew**.

through: in one side, out the other
> trouble spot: th**rough** (not *threw*)
> trick: I th**ough**t I'd b**ough**t en**ough** c**ough** syrup to make it th**rough** this **rough**, t**ough** winter.

till: until
> trouble spot: ti**ll**
> trick: Wait ti**ll** you get the bi**ll**.

to: preposition
> trouble spot: **to** (not *too* or *two*)
> trick: Go **to** the s**to**re.

tobacco: plant leaves used for smoking
> trouble spot: to**b**acco (one **b**)
> trick: Do **b**eer and **c**hocolate **c**hips taste as good as to**bacc**o?

together: as a group
> trouble spot: together
> trick: We went **together to get her**.

tomatoes: kind of fruit
> trouble spot: tomat**oes**
> trick: There were her**oes** facing torped**oes** while eating tomat**oes** and potat**oes**.

tomorrow: day after today
> trouble spot: to**m**orrow (one **m**)
> trick: **Tom** will hu**rr**y and do it **tom**orrow.

tongue: organ used for taste and speech
> trouble spot: tong**ue**
> trick: Don't put gl**ue** on your tong**ue**.

too: also
> trouble spot: **too** (not *to* or *two*)
> trick: Did you break your t**oo**th, t**oo**?

Tow the stalled cow.

torpedoes: underwater projectiles
> trouble spot: torped**oes**
> trick: There were her**oes** facing torped**oes** while eating tomat**oes** and potat**oes**.

tough: difficult; strong
> trouble spot: t**ough**
> trick: I th**ough**t I'd b**ough**t en**ough** c**ough** syrup to make it thr**ough** this r**ough**, t**ough** winter.

tow: to pull
> trouble spot: t**ow** (not *toe*)
> trick: T**ow** the stalled c**ow**.

toward: in the direction of
> trouble spot: to**war**d
> trick: We're moving to**war**d **war**.

tragedy: disaster
> trouble spot: tra**ge**dy (no **d** between **a** and **g**)
> trick: This is an **age** of tra**ge**dy.

transferred: moved
> trouble spot: transf**err**ed
> trick: I was transf**err**ed in **err**or.

treacherous: traitorous
> trouble spot: tr**eacher**ous
> trick: The t**eacher** wasn't tr**eacher**ous.

trespass: transgress
>trouble spot: tre**sp**ass
>trick: **T**re**sp**ass means tran**sg**ress.

trouble: misfortune
>trouble spot: tr**ou**ble
>trick: **Ou**r tr**ou**bles are **y**our tr**ou**bles.

troupe: a group of actors or singers
>trouble spot: tr**oupe** (silent **e**; not *troop*)
>trick: **Ou**r tr**oupe pe**rforms.

truly: really
>trouble spot: tru**ly** (no **e** between **l** and **y**)
>trick: I'll love you tru**ly** in **J**u**ly**.

Tuesday: day of the week
>trouble spot: T**ue**sday
>trick: **Tuesday** is bl**uesday**.

turkey: fowl
>trouble spot: tur**ke**y
>trick: A tur**key** is the **key** to a Thanksgiving dinner.

twelfth: the one after *eleventh*
>trouble spot: twe**lf**th
>trick: The twe**lf**th **elf** was here.

two: number
>trouble spot: **tw**o (silent **w**; not *to* or *too*)
>trick: There are **tw**o **tw**ins.

tying: binding
>trouble spot: t**yi**ng (no **e** between **y** and **i**)
>trick: The dog is cr**ying** while I'm t**ying** it up.

tyranny: an oppressive form of government
>trouble spot: tyra**nn**y (contrast with *tyrant*)
>trick: **Y** (why) isn't tyra**nn**y fu**nn**y?

uncontrollable: not subject to control
    trouble spot: uncontro**ll**able
    trick: This **troll** is uncontro**ll**able.

underrate: estimate too low
    trouble spot: und**err**ate
    trick: It's an **err**or to und**err**ate.

undoubtedly: certainly
    trouble spot: undoub**ted**ly
    trick: **Ted** undoub**ted**ly is the best choice.

university: an educational institution
    trouble spot: univer**sit**y
    trick: Scholars **sit** at the univer**sit**y.

unnecessary: not needed
    trouble spot: u**nn**ecessary
    trick: (Nay-Sayers, page 121)

until: up to the time of
    trouble spot: unti**l** (one **l**)
    trick: "Un**til** the World **Til**ts," a new soap opera.

usage: treatment
    trouble spot: u**sa**ge (no **e** between **s** and **a**)
    trick: The **sage** explained u**sage**.

useful: helpful
    trouble spot: usefu**l** (one **l**)
    trick: One **l** is usefu**l** enough.

using: employing
    trouble spot: u**si**ng (no **e** between **s** and **i**)
    trick: **Sing**, u**sing** your best voice.

Ah, Utah!

usually: most often
    trouble spot: usu**ally**
    trick: Usu**ally** S**ally** answers first.

Utah: U.S. state
    trouble spot: U**tah**
    trick: **Ah**, U**tah**!

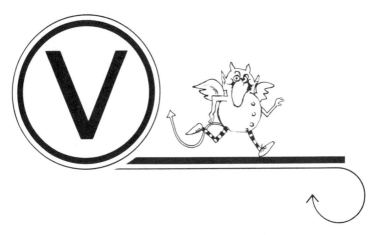

vaccine: a substance injected into the body in order to prevent disease
   trouble spot: va**cc**ine
   trick: How many **cc**'s (**c**ubic **c**entimeters) of the vaccine do you need?

vacuum: cleaning machine
   trouble spot: va**cuu**m (one **c**)
   trick: Pronounce *vacuum* "va–cu–um."

vanilla: a flavoring
   trouble spot: vani**ll**a
   trick: Vani**ll**a makes me **ill**.

various: different
   trouble spot: var**iou**s
   trick: **I o** (owe) **u** (you) var**iou**s gifts.

vary: change
   trouble spot: v**a**ry (not *very*)
   trick: M**ary** won't v**ary**.

vegetable: plant
   trouble spot: ve**get**able
   trick: We **get** ve**get**able**s** when we're **able**.

vengeance: revenge
    trouble spot: veng**ea**nce
    trick: Pronounce *vengeance* "ven–ge–ance."

veteran: person of long experience
    trouble spot: vete**ran**
    trick: The vete**ran**'s term **ran** out.

veterinarian: animal doctor
    trouble spot: vet**erin**arian
    trick: We took our bird, **P**eter, **in** to see **a** veterina**rian**.

vicinity: proximity
    trouble spot: vi**c**inity
    trick: There's a lot of **vice** in this **vic**inity.

vicious: evil
    trouble spot: vi**cious**
    trick: As your **vic**tim, **I o** (owe) **u** (you) a **vicious** blow.

victim: someone harmed by someone or something
    trouble spot: victim
    trick: **Tim** is a vic**tim**.

villain: evildoer
    trouble spot: vi**llain**
    trick: The v**illain** got **ill** in the **rain**.

visible: subject to being seen
    trouble spot: vis**ible**
    trick: Is your s**ibl**ing vis**ible**?

vitamin: organic substance
    trouble spot: vitamin
    trick: I'll take a vita**min in** a **min**ute.

volume: loudness
    trouble spot: vol**ume**
    trick: Is the vol**ume** too high for **u** (you) and **me**?

wail: cry
> trouble spot: **wail** (not *whale* or *wale*)
> trick: When you **ail**, **wail**.

waist: part of the human body
> trouble spot: **waist** (not *waste*)
> trick: The **wait**er has a narrow **wais**t.

ware: product
> trouble spot: **ware** (not *wear* or *where*)
> trick: Put the **war ware**s in the **ware**house.

waste: squander
> trouble spot: **waste** (not *waist*)
> trick: Don't **waste** the **paste** in **haste**.

wealth: riches
> trouble spot: wealth
> trick: W**eal**th can't h**eal** you.

wear: have on the body
> trouble spot: **wear** (not *ware* or *where*)
> trick: W**ear** an **ear**muff.

weather: condition of the atmosphere
> trouble spot: **wea**ther (not *whether*)
> trick: **We eat her** food in all **wea**ther.

Wednesday: day of the week
    trouble spot: We**dnes**day
    trick: Pronounce *Wednesday* "Wed–nes–day."

weigh: to determine the weight or mass of something
    trouble spot: w**eigh** (not *way*)
    trick: Our n**eigh**bor's **eigh**t b**eig**e r**ei**ndeer w**eigh**ed too much to send by fr**eigh**t.

weird: strange
    trouble spot: w**ei**rd
    trick: N**ei**ther l**ei**sured for**eig**n counterf**ei**ter could s**ei**ze **ei**ther w**ei**rd h**ei**ght without forf**ei**ting prot**ei**n.

welcome: greet
    trouble spot: welcome (one l)
    trick: W**el**come the **el**f.

wharf: dock
    trouble spot: w**harf**
    trick: The w**harf** is at the **har**bor.

where: at what place
    trouble spot: **where** (not *ware* or *wear*)
    trick: W**here** is **here**?

whether: in case
    trouble spot: w**he**ther (not *weather*)
    trick: I don't know **whe**ther or **whe**n I will come.

which: what ones
    trouble spot: wh**ich** (not *witch*)
    trick: Wh**ich** r**ich** person was it?

whole: entire
    trouble spot: **wh**ole (not *hole*)
    trick: **Who** knows the **who**le story?

wholly: entirely
    trouble spot: who**ll**y (no **e** between l and l; not *holey* or *holy*)
    trick: Mo**lly** is who**lly** responsible.

whose: belonging to which person
    trouble spot: who**se** (not *who's*)
    trick: **Whose hose** is it?

wintry: of winter
    trouble spot: win**tr**y (no **e** between **t** and **r**)
    trick: **Try** a win**tr**y sport.

witch: woman with magical powers
    trouble spot: **witch** (not *which*)
    trick: A **witch** can make you **itch**.

wrap: enclose
    trouble spot: **wr**ap (not *rap*)
    trick: After I **wr**ap the package, should I **wr**ite the address on it?

wring: squeeze
    trouble spot: **w**ring (not *ring*)
    trick: **W**ring out the **w**ash.

writing: composing
    trouble spot: wri**ti**ng (no **e** between **t** and **i**)
    trick: Your wri**ti**ng makes me **ti**ngle.

written: composed
    trouble spot: wri**tt**en
    trick: What's wri**tt**en on your m**itt**en?

xylophone: musical instrument
    trouble spot: **xy**lophone
    trick: **X, y** (no **z**) **lo phone** is the way you spell **xylophone**.

Did Bach own a yacht?

yacht: pleasure ship
>trouble spot: y**ach**t
>trick: Did B**ach** own a y**ach**t?

yeoman: a petty officer
>trouble spot: yeoman
>trick: Pronounce *yeoman* "ye–o–man."

yield: to turn over
>trouble spot: y**ie**ld
>trick: Y**ie**ld, or d**ie**!

yolk: yellow part of the egg
>trouble spot: yo**lk** (not *yoke*)
>trick: My f**olks** ate the y**olks**.

your: possessive pronoun
>trouble spot: y**our** (not *you're*)
>trick: Y**our** life is not **our** life.

you're: contraction of *you are*
>trouble spot: y**ou're** (not *your*)
>trick: Check **you're** by substituting **you are** to see if the sentence still makes sense.

zenith: highest point
    trouble spot: **z**enith (not **x**)
    trick: **Z**igzag to the **z**enith of the hill.

zinc: metal
    trouble spot: zin**c**
    trick: **Z**in**c** can be mixed with **c**opper.

A Dozen
Spelling Rules

English spelling is, for the most part, illogical and capriciously crazy. If it weren't, there would be no need for mnemonics.

It's important to note, though, that some regularities do exist. Spelling experts over the ages have propounded scores of rules that aim to clarify the fragile patterns. Many of these rules, alas, are so complex that they defy comprehension or memorization. Others have more exceptions than not.

But a few are serviceable. On the following pages a dozen rules that are the most helpful in combatting demons are presented. One hint in reading the rules: Go slow! Even the most valuable spelling rule looks like spaghetti if you try to speed-read it. Take your time. Try to relate the examples to the general statements.

C-Enders

When **c** is the last letter of a word, it is always hard; that is, it is pronounced like a **k**. When adding **-ing**, **-er**, or **-y** to such words, first insert a **k**:

panic—panic**k**y
picnic—picnic**k**ing
traffic—traffic**k**ing

The **k** is said to "protect" the hard sound of the **c**. Without the **k**, the **c** might appear to have a soft sound (**s**) as it does in a word like *icing*.

Note that you don't add the **k** when the suffix begins with a consonant. When adding **-ing** to *mimic,* for example, it becomes *mimicking.* But when **-ry** is added, *mimic* becomes *mimicry* (the **k** is not needed to protect the **c** in this case).

Compounders

When spelling a compound word—a word formed from two other words—keep both words whole. Do not drop the last letter of the first word. Do not drop the first letter of the last word. Simply push the two words together.

side + walk = sidewalk

This rule holds even when the resulting compound word has a strange-looking double letter in the middle.

book + keeper = boo**kk**eeper
ear + ring = ea**rr**ing
hitch + hiker = hitc**hh**iker
news + stand = new**ss**tand
over + rate = ove**rr**ate
room + mate = roo**mm**ate
with + hold = wit**hh**old

A classic exception to this rule is *pastime*:

pass + time = pastime (one **s**; one **t**)

You will find a mnemonic for *pastime* in this book.

Contract'ns

Since many contractions have homonyms, mixups are common. Be sure you have the right word: they're/there/their; we're/were. The trick is to expand the contraction to be certain that you have the right word. Suppose you wrote:

I gave the dog *it's* bone.

Try expanding *it's*. You get:

I gave the dog *it is* bone.

The *it is* obviously makes no sense here. Thus, the correct word is *its*.

Remember to put the apostrophe in the right place. The apostrophe goes in the spot where the letters were omitted. Again, expanding the contraction is the test to make. Suppose you wrote *are'nt*. Check it by expansion: *are'nt = are not*. The **o** in *not* is dropped in making this contraction. That means the apostrophe should go between the **n** and the **t**. Hence, the correct spelling is *aren't*.

Double-Enders

When the last two letters of a single-syllable word are a vowel followed by a consonant, double the consonant before adding a suffix.

rip—ri**pp**er, ri**pp**ing
swim—swi**mm**er, swi**mm**ing
top—to**pp**ing, to**pp**ed

The same rule holds for multiple-syllable words when the final syllable is accented.

acquit—acqui**tt**al
control—contro**ll**ing
submit—submi**tt**ing

Note that words like *seat* become *seating* (one **t**) because there are two vowels before the final consonant. Words like *help* become *helping* (one **p**) because they end in two consonants. And words like *benefit* become *benefited* (one **t**) because they are not accented on the final syllable.

E-Enders

Many words end in a silent **e**. Two rules govern what happens to this **e** when you add suffixes.

First rule: Drop the **e** when the suffix begins with a vowel—**-ed, -ing, -ous, -able, -y.**

lose—losing
louse—lousy
nerve—nervous
prove—provable
tease—teasing

Important exceptions to this rule are *noticeable* and *courageous.* Also, with many words that end in **ve,** it is permissible to either drop or keep the **e** before **-able.**

love—lovable, loveable
move—movable, moveable

Second rule: Keep the silent **e** when the suffix begins with a consonant—**-ment, -ful, -ly.**

care—careful
move—movement

Judgment and *acknowledgment* (no **e**) were once exceptions to this rule, but now *judgement* and *acknowledgement* (with the **e**) are accepted. Two more demonic exceptions—*truly* and *ninth*—drop the expected **e**'s. You'll find mnemonics for each of them in this book.

Ful-Enders

Here's a truth that's short and sweet and very power**ful.** Words that end in **-ful** and mean "full of" always conclude **-ful** (one **l**): *helpful, insightful, sorrowful.* There are no exceptions. Isn't that wonder**ful**?

I Before E (and vice versa)

The most famous spelling rule of all is a jingle that goes like this: *I* before *e* except after *c* or when sounded as *a* as in *neighbor* or *weigh*.

i before e	except after c	sounded as a
lie	conceive	reindeer
thief	receive	rein
field	deceive	inveigle
yield	receipt	heinous

There is a problem with this classic truth. There are at least ten exceptions that "prove" this rule; the mnemonic for them is: **N**either l**ei**sured for**ei**gn counterf**ei**ter could s**ei**ze **ei**ther w**ei**rd h**ei**ght without forf**ei**ting prot**ei**n.

Ly-Enders

When the suffix **-ly** is added to a word, that root word usually stays the same. Hence:

clear—**clear**ly
sincere—**sincere**ly
slow—**slow**ly
undoubted—**undoubted**ly

Two well-known exceptions are: *truly* (from *true*) and *wholly* (from *whole*). You'll find mnemonics for both words in this book.

This (partial) **-ly** truth is especially helpful when facing demons that end in **-lly**.

conceptual—**conceptual**ly
hopeful—**hopeful**ly

When you're not sure if a word ends in **-lly**, try to find the root. For example, *practically* comes from *practical*. The **-ly** is simply tacked on the end.

Nay-Sayers

Nearly a dozen prefixes turn root words into their opposites.

able—**un**able
adjust—**mal**adjust
possible—**im**possible
sense—**non**sense

The root never changes when a negative prefix is added. In *misshape* and *unnatural,* the double letters up front may look strange, but the rule holds firm. All you have to know for sure is how the root word begins.

Suppose, for example, you have written *unecessary* (one **n**). Is that correct? You know the word means "not necessary." *Necessary* is the root. To turn it into its antonym, you must add the prefix **un-**. Hence *unnecessary* (two **n**'s) is the right spelling. Ditto for *illegal* ("not legal"), *misspell* ("spell wrongly"), and *immature* ("not mature").

Occasionally, you'll have a bit of trouble figuring out the root. *Innocent,* for example, is based on *in—nocent* (*nocent* being Latin for "harmed"). Usually, though, the roots will be apparent and you'll know to add the prefix.

    illegible—il**legible**
    irreligious—ir**religious**

The Nay-Sayers' truth should also help you with words like *imagination* (one **m**). This is not a negative form; *agination* is not a word.

Ness-Enders

When adding the suffix **-ness** to a root word, simply add the suffix. The root does not change unless it ends in **y** (happy—happiness). (See Y-Enders below.)

    close—**close**ness
    helpful—**helpful**ness

Remembering that the root does not change will help you defeat mean-looking demons such as:

    mean—**mean**ness
    sudden—**sudden**ness

O-Enders

Rules about plurals seem to multiply. Luckily, plurals don't cause many problems. Nouns that end in **o**, however, can be demonic. The following observations may help.

If a vowel comes before the final **o**, simply add **s**:

radio—radios
rodeo—rodeos

If a consonant comes before the final **o**, usually add **es**:

hero—heroes
potato—potatoes

However, the plural forms of *mosquito* and *tornado* can go either way—**s** or **es**.

There is one general exception. The plural of most music-related **o**-ending words is formed by adding **s** only.

piano—pianos
solo—solos

Y-Enders

When a word ends in **y,** change the **y** to **i** before adding the suffixes **-ly**, **-ness**, or **-age**. You can slay some of the worst demons using this rule.

busy—business
day—daily

easy—easily
empty—emptiness
jerk—jerkily
lonely—loneliness
penny—penniless
marry—marriage
satisfactory—satisfactorily
temporary—temporarily

There are only a few exceptions, such as:

shy—shyly
sly—slyly

Remember to keep the **y** when adding **-ing** (even though it may look a little odd).

Get Published!

Demonic Mnemonics doesn't include all of the difficult-to-spell words in the English language. And some of the mnemonics for words that are included may not work for you. But this book will be updated from time to time, and you can have a part in it. If you have some especially good mnemonics for words, already in the book or not, write them on this page, cut it out, and mail it to Fearon Teacher Aids, Pitman Learning, Inc., 1850 Ralston Avenue, Belmont, California 94002. If any of your mnemonics are used in the revision, you'll get credit as a contributor and a free copy of the book.

Word: _____

Trouble spot: _____

Trick: _____

Word: _____

Trouble spot: _____

Trick: _____

Word: _____

Trouble spot: _____

Trick: _____

Word: _____

Trouble spot: _____

Trick: _____

Your name: _____

Your address/city/state/zip code: _____